W9-APQ-917

PIONEER WOMEN

The Lives of Women
on the Frontier

PIONEER WOMEN

The Lives of Women
on the Frontier

~ Linda Peavy & Ursula Smith ~

SMITHMARK

Above: At the request of Lady Evelyn Cameron, an English immigrant whose photographs conveyed the spirit of everyday life in the West, this unidentified couple posed in front of their dugout on the Dragseth Ranch in eastern Montana.

Page 1: A Montana horsewoman.

To the pioneer women who lived the history they told and to the scholars who have dedicated their lives and energies to writing those women into history—especially all our colleagues in the Coalition for Western Women's History.

Copyright © 1996, Saraband Inc.
Design © Ziga Design
Text © Linda Peavy and Ursula Smith

Editor: Julia Banks Rubel
Photo editor: Sara Hunt
Photo researchers: Gillian Speeth,
   Emily Head
Illustrations: © 1995 Donna Ruff

A *Saraband* BOOK

All rights reserved. No part of this publication may be reproduced, stored in a retrieval system or transmitted in any form by any means electronic, mechanical, photocopying or otherwise, without first obtaining written permission of the copyright owner.

This edition published in 1996 by Smithmark Publishers, a division of US Media Holdings, Inc., 16 East 32nd Street, New York, NY 10016.

SMITHMARK books are available for bulk purchase for sales, promotion, and premium use. For details, write or call the manager of special sales, SMITHMARK Publishers, 16 East 32nd Street, New York, NY 10016 (212) 532-6600.

Produced by: Saraband Inc, PO Box 0032, Rowayton, CT 06853-0032.

ISBN: 0-8317-7220-4

Printed in China

10 9 8 7 6 5 4 3

TABLE OF CONTENTS

Introduction

In February 1864, Pamelia Fergus of Little Falls, Minnesota, loaded her belongings—and her four children—into two ox-drawn wagons and traveled south, bound for Henry County, Illinois, where she planned to spend a few weeks visiting with her mother before she turned her wagons west and headed for Virginia City, Montana Territory, to join her husband, James.

Shortly after her arrival in Illinois, Pamelia wrote a letter to James detailing the luxuries she was enjoying there, luxuries that had been sorely missed during her nine years in frontier Minnesota, luxuries that she would leave behind again when she crossed the plains and moved into the log cabin James had built in the Rocky Mountain mining camp that would be her new home. "If we had our house here in this country," she wrote, "I should want to stay. I have lived a mong the Indians and the frountears long enough."

Fergus's sentiments are understandable, for she had, indeed, spent most of her life "a mong the Indians and the frountears." Born in 1824 in a skeletal settlement in upstate New York, Pamelia Dillin had grown up as a child of that early frontier. At eighteen she had made her first overland emigration, joining her family in a wintertime wagon journey to a farm in Henry County, Illinois, some thousand miles distant. Her subsequent move into the city of Moline and her eventual marriage to James Fergus, a Scottish immigrant with an entrepreneurial bent, had, for a while, introduced her to the benefits of life in a more cultured society. Then, in the spring of 1855, she and her three children had packed up their belongings, boarded a Mississippi River steamboat, and followed James to a pioneer settlement in present-day Minnesota—essentially giving up all the amenities she'd gained.

As though she were moving backward in time, Pamelia had found herself facing once again the burdensome domestic tasks that had been her lot during her frontier childhood. Frustrated by the lack of amenities available to her family in Little Falls, she had enlisted the help of several other women in the community and directed her energies toward the establishment of a church and a school, seeing both institutions as essential to the moral and intellectual development of her children.

Caught up in the spirit of rapid growth, the women of the fledgling community shared the dreams of their husbands. They

Opposite: *With a porcelain bowl for a bathtub and a wood-burning stove for warmth, little Lucille Lippincott seems to have no complaints about growing up in the mining town of Silver City, Idaho, though her mother must have been acutely aware of the privations of frontier living.*

Left: *Eager as she was for reunion with her gold-seeking husband, Minnesota pioneer Pamelia Fergus did not look forward to crossing the plains by ox-drawn wagon and starting all over again on the still farther "frountear" of Virginia City, Montana Territory.*

Opposite, above:
Oregon pioneer Hannah Williams sewed pictures of herself and her husband onto a scrap from the tent used during their overland journey.

Opposite, below:
Using traditional methods, this Sarsi, or Sotemia, tribeswoman of Alberta, Canada, dries food over a fire.

Below: *A detail from Emmanuel Luetz's* Westward the Course of Empire Takes Its Way *reveals the stereotypical "Madonna of the Prairie" image of the nineteenth century.*

planted apple trees and roses and looked forward to bountiful years in which their orchards and gardens would yield abundant fruit and flowers.

But Pamelia's fruit trees were still saplings when a flood, a drought, and a grasshopper plague took their toll on the local economy, bringing her husband's business to the brink of bankruptcy. Inspired by accounts of gold in the Rockies, James Fergus had left his wife and family behind and headed west in search of the funds he needed to pay off his debts. Now, after four years of managing things on her own while intermittent letters kept her apprised of her husband's activities in the West, Pamelia had finally received a letter indicating that James was ready for her to sell off their Little Falls properties, pack up their belongings, and bring the children west.

Although she was eager to have the family reunited and heartened by her husband's glowing reports of life in Virginia City,

Pamelia dreaded the thought of yet another move. It seemed she had endured a lifetime of pioneering already. The move to Montana Territory promised to be the most drastic of all, for she would be traveling to a still farther "frountear," moving so far back in time and so deep into wilderness that she must have had serious doubts as to whether civilization as she had all-too-briefly known it would ever catch up with her.

The Fabric of History

One of the thousands of pioneer women who helped settle the American West, Pamelia Fergus would no doubt be quite surprised to find that her experiences—so long considered unworthy of mention—have finally become the stuff of history, have indeed been recorded in some detail in a book, *The Gold Rush Widows of Little Falls*, and have even been immortalized in song in the opera *Pamelia*.

Her surprise would be understandable, for during her lifetime—and until the last third of the twentieth century—frontier history was seen as *his*-story, a lively and entertaining account of the deeds of the male explorers, soldiers, miners, farmers, cattle barons, and politicians who made their way westward after European settlers had claimed the eastern shores of this continent as their own. Pioneering women, if mentioned at all, were dismissed as bit players in the drama of the ever-expanding frontier.

Those American mythmakers who did manage to add a feminine figure to the western scene generally chose to depict her as one of two broad types. She could be some variation of the Madonna of the Prairie—the faithful helpmeet, the "gentle tamer," a lady of some refinement who, though resigned to her harsh lot of monotonous drudgery, was determined to ensure her children a better life by imposing her version of civilization on the wilderness. Alternatively, she was the antithesis of that stereotype—the backwoods belle, the soiled dove, the female bandit, a woman of unsavory character, although perhaps less one-dimensional than her pure and passive counterpart.

Introduction

Recent studies of women on the trail, of women homesteaders, and of women left to cope on their own in frontier environments have begun to broaden our concept of pioneering women. Though there is still much work to be done, these studies have, in the words of historian Susan Armitage, enabled us to begin to put together a patchwork quilt made up of scraps from the lives of many pioneer women, and a careful study of the many different squares in this quilt should give us a fairly good idea of what it was like to be a woman of the American frontier.

The very diversity of those squares—some of them dark and somber, others bright with promise and hope, some of them marred by the ragged stitches of women barely able to carry on, others enriched by the precise handwork of women clearly in control of their lives and circumstance—is a reminder of the importance of paying attention to the specifics, the particulars that set each woman's experiences apart from those of her neighbors.

Unfortunately, most of us know far too little about the lives of the Native American neighbors of early frontier settlers. This is not surprising, since most of the writers whose works have formed our basic perceptions about the experiences of those early cultures were Euro-Americans whose writings tended to depict all people of different cultures as "the other" or to ignore them altogether, unless their presence and practices happened to interfere with—or assist in—the pursuit of this country's Manifest Destiny. And, since those Anglo writers were also almost exclusively male, the women of those "other" cultures were afforded even less attention than the men.

Furthermore, many otherwise excellent studies of pioneer women have been almost as anglocentric as those earlier, more general histories, focusing as they do almost exclusively on the experiences of the nineteenth-century white women involved in the westward migration and containing few, if any, references to the experiences of the Native American women whose lives were so drastically altered by that migration. This

Right: Pueblo, Colorado pioneers William Johnson, Iva Melton, and Laura Bell show off a litter of pups—all of them destined to become fine hunting dogs.

seems particularly ironic in view of the fact that the Indians encountered by settlers moving west were, themselves, the descendants of this continent's *very* earliest immigrants—the prehistoric wanderers who first peopled its mountains and plains.

The experiences of women of all cultures deserve careful study, and though a truly multicultural history of the women of the American West is clearly beyond the scope of this book, wherever possible, accounts of the day-to-day experiences of Hispanic, Anglo, African American, and Asian pioneer women will be set against the experiences of the Native American women whose lives were affected by the westward movement.

Those of us attempting to construct a realistic history of westering women must honor the shapes of the lives we chronicle, and since the stories of women's lives tend to be stories of dailiness, rather than stories of singular events, the stories in this book differ in tone and emphasis from the heroic sagas of westering men found in more traditional histories. This is entirely appropriate if one agrees with Susan Armitage's assertion that "[just] because some men in western history have achieved heroic stature" is no reason to "think that we need to create female figures in the same mold." And, if one accepts her conclusion that "[since] even the most heroic people lead ordinary lives 99 percent of the time… [then] ordinary lives are the true

story of the West, for men as well as for women," then learning about the everyday lives of a representative number of pioneer women can give us a far greater understanding of the frontier experience as a whole than we might gain, say, from a careful study of the heroic exploits of any one person—male or female.

As Colorado pioneer May Wing told historian Elizabeth Jameson, "I lived the history that I…tell." And it is that history, history written or told by those who lived it, that we have chosen to feature in *Pioneer Women*. Drawing upon unpublished diaries, memoirs, and letters as well as upon the growing number of such papers that have found their way into print, we have sought to let these women speak for themselves.

Right: Details gleaned from the letters and diaries of pioneer women can be pieced into a patchwork quilt depicting life on the far frontier.

Introduction

There are problems with such an approach, for diaries women wrote to share with family members back home are quite different in tone and content from those that were never meant to be read by anyone other than the author herself. Letters, too, are either more or less candid, depending upon whose eyes were likely to fall upon the lines contained therein. Memoirs, often written decades after the experience being described, lack the immediacy and accuracy of accounts written in diaries and letters. And family records left in the archives of libraries or historical societies may have been "purged" before they were deposited there.

Furthermore, primary sources of this type give us access only to the experiences of women who were able to write—the literate few who were able to set down their thoughts on paper. Fortunately, there are other sources that allow a glimpse into the lives of women who left behind no autobiographical writings. Though few and far between, transcripts made by early oral historians who interviewed Native American women are helpful, though often limited in their scope and emphasis. Similarly, transcripts of interviews with Anglo, Hispanic, and African American pioneer women who left no written records of their own can broaden our views of frontier living. And, in the case of women who participated in the Klondike gold rush or the 1930s homesteading endeavors in the Dakotas and the Northwest, tape-recorded interviews made in recent years can give us the sound of the women's voices as well as written transcripts of their narratives. Like memoirs written by the women themselves, transcripts of interviews done many years after the homesteading or gold-seeking days have passed are told in retrospect—and therefore subject to errors of memory and recall.

These cautionary notes having been sounded, since the history these women tell is, indeed, the history they lived, their own words remain our best means of gaining a clear picture of what their lives were like. Filled with quotations from frontier women of many different cultures, many different eras, and many different walks of life, *Pioneer Women* is a patchwork—or better, a patch*word* quilt, a rich and authentic verbal mosaic of pioneer life.

Moving On: A Way of Life

As historian John Mack Faragher has noted, "Americans have always had itching feet," a fact that had led another young historian, Frederick Jackson Turner, to conclude one hundred years earlier that "for nearly three centuries the dominant fact in American life has been expansion." In a sense the colonists themselves were pioneers, since they had left behind the culture of another continent and traveled across an ocean to face the unknown dangers that awaited them on a distant shore. Here many of them met with hardships, deprivations, and dangers—inadequate housing, food shortages, lack of schools and churches and medical care, hostile encounters with indigenous peoples—that are quite similar to those encountered by this country's later pioneers.

Below: *The men and women who explored and settled the American West in the nineteenth and early twentieth centuries faced hardships, dangers, and deprivations similar to those endured by the earliest American colonists.*

Right: *This 1875 engraving from* Frank Leslie's Illustrated Newspaper *depicts daily life in the large barracks that Russian Mennonites in central Kansas erected to shelter incoming settlers until they could build suitable dugouts and soddies for themselves and their families.*

Right: *This 1875 engraving from* Frank Leslie's Illustrated Newspaper *depicts daily life in the large barracks that Russian Mennonites in central Kansas erected to shelter incoming settlers until they could build suitable dugouts and soddies for themselves and their families.*

In this same sense, the earliest settlers to move away from the relative safety of established communities—either in search of religious freedom or of greater and better land holdings—were also pioneers, and the experiences of the women among them often mirror the experiences of the women most often associated with stories of the westward migration. Moving on in the early days of this country's history meant moving in any direction where land had not already been claimed and settled by others. At first these settlers made some effort to avoid encroaching on the lands of Native American peoples, preferring to keep the peace whenever possible. But as the number of settlers grew and the Indians began to retreat in the face of enticing treaties and vicious attacks, increasing numbers of pioneers began to make their way beyond the established boundaries of the early colonies, following migration routes south, north, and west.

Rebecca Bryan Boone was such a pioneer. Described by an early biographer as "an instrument ordained to settle the wilderness," Daniel Boone became the symbol of early exploration, and his wife soon learned to expect that as soon as her wandering husband returned home with news that the lands ahead were safe for women and children, she would be obliged to make yet another move into the wilderness. Each move had its own triumphs and tragedies, but her move to Kentucky was, perhaps, the most traumatic of all.

That move, accomplished shortly after the birth of her eighth child in 1773, involved a long trek by horseback along a rough trace barely wide enough for the horses to traverse in single file. According to details provided by an early resident of the area, the Boones had "prepared baskets made of fine hickory withe or splints, and fastening two of them together with ropes, they put a child in each basket and put it across a pack saddle." Carrying their poultry in the same kind of baskets, Rebecca and Daniel Boone drove cattle and hogs before them with the help of their eldest children and the various relatives and friends who had chosen to cast their lot with the famous explorer.

While this legendary journey into Kentucky Territory has long been viewed as a triumph, it was, in fact, a blatant encroachment upon lands occupied by the Cherokees and Shawnees. The Boone family paid dearly for ignoring warnings issued earlier by the two tribes, for sixteen-year-old James Boone, who had been sent back to a trading post for additional provisions, was tortured and killed by a party of Delaware, Shawnee, and Cherokee warriors.

Introduction

Left: *The opening of the Union Pacific's western line meant safer, faster travel, and many women who had been reluctant to cross the plains by wagon made the journey west by rail.*

In time, travel beyond the boundaries of the early colonies became somewhat easier than it had been for the Boone family. By 1803 the federal government had already adopted a policy of using monies from the sale of public lands to build roadways that would help move people and goods across the eastern portion of the continent, and by 1818 the National Road was completed from Cumberland, Maryland, on the Potomac all the way to Wheeling, West Virginia, on the Ohio River. Soon thereafter the Lancaster Pike was expanded westward as far as Pittsburgh, and Americans who chose to do so could find land of their own by following roads that led beyond the boundaries of the nation's earliest towns and cities. As more and more citizens took advantage of the new routes, the influx of settlers sent Daniel Boone farther westward—into the wilds of Missouri—where he and Rebecca and several of their children lived out their days in relative isolation.

Even as Boone went into retirement, new leaders were taking up his challenge and setting out to forge new trails across the Northwest Territory and beyond. With the nation's population having doubled between 1800 and 1820, the lure of better and cheaper lands to the west caused further emigration. Many families followed the Ohio River to its farthest point west, and after the completion of the Erie Canal in 1825, many more chose that water route west, leaving the canal at Lake Erie and setting out from there with their wagons, handcarts, or packhorses, searching always for the perfect homesite in present-day Michigan, Indiana, Illinois, Iowa, or Missouri.

Prior to 1840 the female population in the West included Native American and Hispanic women, a few brave Anglo females who had accompanied the many men along the Santa Fe Trail to New Mexico, and a few more who had gone west with fur

Below: *In this 1874* Harper's Weekly *sketch of travelers fording a river, former slaves join Anglo emigrants in the search for a new home on the frontier.*

Above: In most mining settlements, women were in short supply and great demand, as seen in this newspaper sketch in which a lonely male laments, "O Sally, how you'd pity me could you behold me now."

Right: In this 1884 sketch, residents of a mining camp in the Coeur d'Alene area of northern Idaho celebrate the arrival of the town's first female citizen.

traders and explorers. However, for the most part, before 1840, the trans-Mississippi West was, as Susan Armitage has observed, primarily *His* land. Not until rumors of the availability of free land in the Northwest set off a mass migration to Oregon Territory—which was, at that time, a vast area stretching all the way from the Pacific Coast to the Continental Divide—did Anglo women begin to move west in substantial numbers. By that time, news that missionary couples—notably Narcissa and Marcus Whitman—had made the journey and were working among the Indians of Oregon Territory inspired many heretofore wary families to dare the trip themselves.

The Great Migration of 1843, the first to reach the Willamette Valley, boasted a goodly number of women among the thousand-plus pioneers who set out to find a new life in the West, a venture journalist Horace Greeley described as wearing "an aspect of insanity." Most of the families on that trek were part of a fairly large group historians have labeled "movers," people who had been pushing boundaries ever since their arrival on this continent, driven by the same hunger for land that had led them to leave the British Isles or northern Europe in hopes of gaining a bit of earth for themselves and their families. In the old world, the ownership of land had been the single most important distinction between poverty and economic success, and when the acquisition of farms became too difficult in one place, these movers

were the first to break up housekeeping and set off chasing still another dream.

Now, with the passage of the first Preemption Act in 1842, farmers who improved the land could be fairly sure of owning that land one day. And with news of the introduction of a new bill that would give 640 acres to every male citizen over the age of eighteen and 160 acres each to his wife and his children, wagons began to queue up at frontier towns along the Mississippi and Missouri Rivers. Confident that if this bill did not pass as written—and ultimately it did not—some other bill would soon offer similar enticements, men were ready to risk the difficult crossing in order to be able to claim whatever acreage was made available to them. Typical of such men was Peter Burnett of Missouri, who sought to convince his wife to join him in the quest by asserting, "Out in Oregon I can get me a square mile of land. And a quarter section for each of you all. Dad burn me, I am done with this country. Winters it's frost and snow to freeze a body; summers the overflow from Old Muddy drowns half my acres; taxes take the yield of them that's left. Maw, it's God's country."

The responses women had to such appeals were many and varied, as their diaries and those of their daughters attest. Martha Gay Masterson, who was thirteen when her family crossed the plains in the spring of 1851, belonged to a family of

Introduction

"movers." Over the first twenty-three years of his marriage, her father, Martin Gay, had led his family from Kentucky to Tennessee to Missouri to Arkansas and then back to Missouri before finally setting out for Oregon. Her mother, Ann, then pregnant with her twelfth child, was understandably reluctant to undertake this final journey but eventually consented and did her part in readying the family for the trip. Ann Gay's attitude toward the crossing was shared by many other women who were torn between concern for the safety of their families and an awareness that their husbands were probably right to assume that there were better opportunities out west. At any rate, in most cases the women knew the decision to go west had already been made.

The Great Migration of 1843 was memorable because these settlers broke trail, so to speak, and their success in the venture gave hope to the thousands of emigrants who followed in their wake. But that migration was hardly unique. The women who went to Oregon or California in 1843—and all of those who went west in the years thereafter—had, like the emigrants to this country's earliest frontiers, left well-established homes and farms behind them and traveled to unsettled regions where they were obliged to begin all over again the process of setting up housekeeping and doing what they could to improve living conditions by starting schools, churches, theatres, and social organizations similar to the ones they'd left behind. Thus, though there are striking differences in the experiences of pioneers of different eras, there are also important similarities. By putting into historical perspective the words and deeds of ordinary women whose day-to-day labors made a significant, if quiet, contribution to the settling of the American West, *Pioneer Women* is, in a sense, paying tribute to the extraordinariness of ordinary lives.

The ordinary lives detailed on these pages have a drama all their own, if one only senses the tension underlying their struggles against hunger and cold, illness and ignorance, prejudice and violence. And the primary actors in these day-to-day scenes were often women, women who by and large accepted the struggle and deprivation as just another job to be done. Ordinary women, who, like Pamelia Fergus, would no doubt be quite surprised to find that their lives have, at long last, come to be seen as the stuff of history.

Above: *Though hardly an ideal place to birth a child, this lean-to and tent provided shelter for a family staking its claim to a town lot in Guthrie in 1889, the year Indian Territory became Oklahoma Territory and was opened to Anglo settlement.*

The Journey West

Pioneer Women on the Move

Soon after the earliest wagon trains went west, guidebooks such as *The Emigrants Guide to Oregon and California* (1845) and *Journal of Travels over the Rocky Mountains* (1846) began to appear in the East and Midwest, providing advice and tips for emigrants preparing for the journey. From these books one could learn how to choose and break stock; how to select or build a wagon; how to outfit that wagon and stock it with clothes, food, and implements; how to set up camp; and how to locate grass and water for stock.

In later years, the discovery of gold in California led to the speedy publication of a second group of guidebooks with titles like *The Emigrant's Guide to the Gold Mines…Together with…Full Instructions upon the Best Method of Getting There, Living, Expenses, etc., etc., and a Complete Description of the Country.* Issued immediately after the California strike, these books not only provided tips for the overland journey west but also discussed the pros and cons of sailing west—around the Horn, across the Isthmus of Panama, or via the Nicaragua route. Subsequent guidebooks written a decade or so after the strikes in Colorado and Idaho Territories provided rail and steamboat itineraries for travelers bound for Pikes Peak or the Salmon River country.

These and virtually all the major guidebooks prior to the 1860s were written by and for men going west without their families. Since men had to eat—with or without their wives at hand to cook for them—most of these guidebooks included at least a few tips concerning the cooking implements essential to life on the trail, but since these books were intended for a small company of men and not for women who were feeding entire families and looking ahead to setting up kitchens in their new homes, they were not particularly useful to women emigrants. Nor did the books contain any tips on making a bed in the wagon or tent, washing dishes and clothes along the trail, or keeping infants dry and clean during those periods when water was too scarce to be used for washing.

Preparing and Packing

Fortunately, most of the women who made the 1843 crossing along what was to become known as the Oregon Trail—and most of the women who followed that trail over the next two decades—were part of that restless segment of American society that had participated in earlier migrations to frontier communities in the Midwest. They knew from experience how to handle cooking and cleaning chores on the trail. They also knew which utensils and household items were indispensable for a journey across the plains and which could be done without.

Faced with yet another time of reckoning, experienced emigrants sold or traded bulky items such as heavy earthenware pots or fireplace tools for camp stoves, wagon wheels, and other items that would be useful on the trail. Faced once again with difficult decisions about which family keepsakes had to be parted with—favorite paintings or pieces of furniture, hand-painted plates, grandma's quilts—they auctioned off some heirlooms and entrusted the rest to friends or relatives.

Even experienced movers like Kitturah Penton Belknap, whose family had earlier

Opposite: Sunbonneted pioneer women watch as wagons from their emigrant train thread their way through a narrow pass.

Above: *Middle-class women accustomed to cooking in well-equipped kitchens such as this one found it hard to give up treasured pots, pans, dishes, and appliances as they prepared for the journey west.*

Right: *In packing wagons bound for Montana Territory, Pamelia Fergus was expected to follow her husband's three-page "Outfit Memorandum" listing everything from "dessicated vegatables" to "woolen mittens."*

emigrated to Iowa, found time running out as the day for departure drew near:

> *I have to make a feather tick for my bed…the linen is ready to go to work on, and six two bushel bags all ready to sew up…have cut out two pair of pants for George…I have worked almost day and night this winter, have the sewing about all done but a coat and vest for George. Will wash and begin to pack and start with some old clothes on and when we can't wear them any longer will leave them on the road.*

At least Belknap's husband was close at hand during her preparations for the journey west. Pamelia Fergus of Little Falls, Minnesota, had been on her own for nearly four years by the time her husband finally sent word that he was ready for the family to join him in the West. Faced with the task of readying herself and her four children for the trip to Montana Territory, Pamelia followed a three-page memorandum from James in gathering the items she was to take on her journey—an extensive list divided into sections titled "Teams," "Provisions," "Clothing," "Stationary," and "Extras for Use on Road."

She was to pack all the belongings from home in a single wagon, which she was to drive as far as Illinois, where she would be met by a partner of James's, O. J. Rockwell, who would provide her with two additional covered wagons, six more yoke of oxen, and a good milk cow. At Council Bluffs, Iowa, her jumping-off spot for the trip across the plains, she was to buy such provisions as James instructed: 600 pounds of flour, 300 of meal, 50 of beans, 100 of rice, 50 of cheese, 50 of butter, and 400 of sugar, plus two barrels of crackers, 20 gallons of syrup, and specified amounts of black tea, coffee, salt, bacon, ham, dried beef, codfish, and dried fruits and vegetables.

Cooking on the trail would require a camp stove, camp kettles, and a tin reflector, plus frying pans. Once they reached Virginia City, Pamelia would find the large cookstove, milk pans, water buckets, a sausage cutter, table dishes, matches, and a half-dozen good brooms that James had waiting for her. He had seen too many cookstoves and other household items abandoned on the trail to consider bringing along anything of significant weight that he could buy for her in the West.

There were, of course, other necessities Pamelia should pack in her wagon, including items James listed under "washing apperatus": a washtub, washboard, two flatirons, starch, soap, and concentrated lye for making soap once she arrived at her new home. She was also to

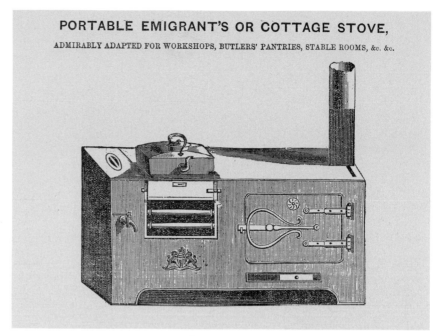

PORTABLE EMIGRANT'S OR COTTAGE STOVE,
ADMIRABLY ADAPTED FOR WORKSHOPS, BUTLERS' PANTRIES, STABLE ROOMS, &c. &c.

bring along "one good strong sewing machine" with an assortment of threads and yarns, plus a heavy-duty needle for sewing buckskin. She was to pack up their feather beds into the smallest possible bundles and wrap them up in two "Indian Rubber Spreads" that she was to place on the ground inside their tent each night before she rolled out the feather beds.

Since he was already well acquainted with the weather in Montana Territory—as well as the weather she could expect to encounter on the plains—James also included detailed lists of clothing for himself, Pamelia, and each of the four children. A man of letters who intended his family's experience to be well recorded, he asked her to bring along two reams of good white letter paper, one ream of foolscap, a half-dozen memorandum books, a book of legal forms, two books of "bill paper," and five dollars' worth of stamped envelopes. Two gold pens for the girls, one box of steel pens and holders, two large

Above: *Though this advertisement for a portable emigrant's stove manufactured in England claims the appliance was "widely exported and found to meet all requirements of a camp stove," it was made of "strong wrought iron" and its weight would have made it less than ideal for a wagon journey.*

Left: *When Pamelia Fergus set out for the West in 1864, she took along this Wheeler & Wilson sewing machine—but failed to follow her husband's suggestion that she treadle her way across the plains, sewing flour sacks to be sold in Montana Territory.*

A Home on Wheels

Known as prairie schooners, the wagons of the 1860s were generally ten feet long, four feet wide, and two feet deep; some of them had false bottoms in which items could be stored. The canvas top—double thick and waterproofed with paint or linseed oil—was stretched over bows that were high enough that a person could stand in the center. Sometimes storage pockets were sewn on the inside of the canvas to hold toilet articles, favorite books, and kitchen cutlery. Goods were packed along the interior sides of the wagon box, leaving a narrow passage down the middle, so that a person could walk along and have relatively easy access to the goods on either side. In some wagons, a favorite rocker occupied that narrow passage, and a few enterprising pioneers crafted beds that could be positioned across the boxes so that the family could sleep inside the wagon at day's end.

The interior of a wagon could be quite elaborate, and homesteader Virginia Ivins described a party traveling with three spring wagons "with folding beds inside, leaving room for small chairs and sewing tables, work baskets, bird cages, and pretty knick knacks around." This was apparently a well-to-do family, for they had brought along "a good girl to do the cooking," and they slept in "an elegant marquee tent." Strapped to the outside of the wagons were buckets of grease for the axles, tools for farming ventures, water barrels, spare wheels and other wagon parts, and whatever furniture was considered irreplacable. Some families were eventually obliged to leave many of these items along the trail, since a fully loaded wagon could weigh fifteen hundred to two thousand pounds and the loss of any draft animal necessitated lightening the load.

While there were differences of opinion as to the best draft animals for such a trip, oxen or mules were generally better able than horses to endure so long and hard a journey. And though two yoke—four oxen—could pull a fully loaded wagon, three yoke were a better bet, since the loss of livestock along the way could jeopardize a family's chances for completing the trip.

Above: *Homesteaders bound for Nebraska.*

bottles of ink, and two dozen lead pencils were also on his list, along with schoolbooks and slates, maps and books for the children's schooling. A box of candles, candle molds and wicking, two lamps with durable chimneys, and a few extra lamp chimneys were also suggested.

Since breakdowns on the trail could prove disastrous, he included a list of emergency items—oxshoe nails, tongue bolts and wagon grease, tar, spirits of turpentine, oxbows, and an extra yoke and chain. They would need whiskey for dosing cattle poisoned by bad water and for making vinegar once they got to Virginia City.

Finally, she was to bring out extra gold pans, a pair of gold scales, and a pair of spectacles for James. Toward construction of their new home, she was to bring some padlocks, two half-boxes of window glaze, two kegs of assorted nails, a few "papers" of assorted screws, and a package of "miners shoe tacks," along with a shovel, pick, and hoe, a half-dozen handsaw files, one flat file, and one bucksaw. A request for assorted ammunition—five boxes of cartridges, shot, powder, and caps—completed James's list of necessities.

Toward her preparations for the family's trip, James sent his wife four hundred dollars in gold dust. He sent an additional five hundred dollars to his partner Rockwell, who was to purchase their additional wagons, livestock, and provisions. Lest Pamelia fret herself over not being able to follow all of his directions, James assured her, "If some of these articles should be forgotten it will not matter a great deal because they can all be purchased here only at higher prices. Don't fret yourself about anything. Do your best and let the rest go."

Modes of Travel on the Overland Trail

Most of the homeseeking families who set out for Oregon, Californa, or Utah in the 1840s traveled by wagon, but between 1856 and 1860, when Mormon funds for bringing new converts to Utah Territory grew scarce, hundreds of families walked all the way to the promised land, drawing behind them handcarts that held all their belongings. Unlike the majority of emigrants who had chosen to go west, these were not hearty frontier families used to rural living but were mostly immigrants from factory towns in England. In these "handcart com-

Below: Between 1856 and 1860, thousands of converts from England, Wales, and Scandinavia walked all the way to Utah, pulling five-hundred-pound carts adorned with such slogans as "Zion's Express" and "Truth Will Prevail." This 1850s woodcut of handcart emigrants crossing Iowa captures the high spirits of these zealous travelers, most of whom would have agreed with Priscilla Merriman Evans that this was, indeed, "a glorious way to come to Zion."

Above: *Starvation and cold brought by Wyoming blizzards killed nearly two hundred of the thousand Mormon emigrants in the Martin and Willie handcart companies of 1856. Dozens lost fingers and toes to frostbite, and more would have perished without the aid of rescue parties sent out by Brigham Young.*

Opposite, above: *Robert Lindneux's famous painting of the Trail of Tears. Over four thousand people—about 25 percent of the Cherokee nation—died in the winter of 1838 when U.S. policy forced the tribe to leave their lands in Georgia and march over eight hundred miles into what is now the state of Oklahoma.*

panies," women generally outnumbered men, and many persons of both sexes were elderly. Each handcart could carry four hundred to five hundred pounds, its contents serving four or five persons, and a group of handcarts was generally accompanied by four or five wagons carrying communal food and tents. Since these wagons had no room for passengers, anyone who fell ill and could not walk had to ride atop that family's handcart.

Such a long walk might seem a difficult assignment, but Priscilla Merriman Evans recalled that though there were "a great many who made fun of us as we walked, pulling our carts, …the weather was fine and the roads were excellent and although I was sick [pregnant] and we were tired out at night, we still thought, 'This is a glorious way to come to Zion.'" Her spirit was apparently shared by most of her fellow travelers, for except for some three dozen emigrants who literally walked themselves to death, the families in those first three handcart companies arrived in Salt Lake City in the summer of 1856 in remarkably good condition.

As Evans noted, generally the weather was, indeed, fine for her company and the other two that began the journey west within the narrow window of time—April 15 to May 30—considered safe for departures. Two other handcart companies who were late in forming up decided—against the advice of experienced travelers—to

forge ahead despite their tardy departure date. More than two hundred of the one thousand emigrants died in weather-related tragedies, and dozens more lost toes and fingers to frostbite.

Emma Batchelor and Elizabeth Summers, who had sailed from England in the expectation of going directly to Utah, were among those caught in the weather, and Elizabeth lost most of her toes. Sometime later, when Mormon president Brigham Young congratulated Emma for having made the journey in good health, she confessed, "I was one who called out to go when Brother Savage warned us. I was at fault in that," but added,

I tried to make up for it. I pulled my full share at the cart every day. When we came to a stream, I stopped and took off my shoes and stockings and outer skirt and put them on top of the cart. Then after I got the cart across….I sat down and scrubbed my feet hard with my woolen neckerchief and put on dry shoes and stockings.

Despite the suffering and death experienced by the final two handcart parties of that season, the Mormons continued the handcart emigration for another three years, for at approximately twenty-five dollars per person, this form of conveyance made it possible for practically penniless emigrants to join their fellow believers in Zion.

Some emigrants had reason to envy the Mormons and their handcarts. According to historian Sandra Myres, one Mexican-American woman traveled the entire way on horseback, with her toddlers riding in sacks hung on each side of her saddle. Emigrant Maggie Hall reported seeing a party consisting of a man and a boy, each carrying a gun on his shoulder, and "one horse, a feather bed tied on it & woman sat upon it and tied on horse were pans, kittle & little bags, etc."

Myres also reported that a Texas woman recalled putting "all *ouer rament* and things on the old horse," starting with the most delicate things, then adding "ouer pervishan then ouer little kittle which was hard-

ley large enofe to cook a boiled dinner for three person then the Skillet and lid was put on top then my spining wheel." The horse apparently bore his load with great patience until a lame pig was added to the stack on its back, at which point the indignant steed "run off and made a compleet stampeed and kept picking and kicking untell he got everything off and the result was the pigs brains was smasht out and the dinner pot broke all in bits."

Martha Frink wrote in her journal that somewhere in the Humboldt Sink in western Nevada she saw "a Negro woman… tramping along through the heat and dust, carrying a cast iron bake stove on her head, with her provisions and a blanket piled on top…bravely pushing on for California." Biddy Mason, who eventually became quite wealthy through her California real estate dealings but was still a slave at the time she made her overland emigration, walked beside the wagons of her owners all the way from Mississippi to California, "herding sheep much of the way."

Black slaves weren't the only travelers who went west under less than ideal cir-

cumstances. As historian Angie Debo has noted, in the 1830s, Indians forced to leave their homelands in the eastern woodlands and make their way to the dry plains of Oklahoma Territory had no choice as to when or how they traveled. Consequently, the tribes suffered great losses. During their passage west, 45 percent of the Creeks died and 25 percent of the Cherokee nation was lost on the forced march that became known as the Trail of Tears.

Below: An 1897 burro pack train on the Dyea Trail, one of the beginning branches of the popular overland trail to the Klondike.

Left: Celebrating the opening of the first western line through the Alleghenies.

Below: An 1869 poster announcing the long-awaited opening of the Union Pacific's Platte Valley route to the West.

Opposite, above and below: While wealthy passengers enjoyed bountiful meals served in elegantly appointed dining cars and spent their nights in luxurious "Pullman's Palace" sleepers, most emigrant families ate from baskets or boxes of home-made fare and slept on the wooden seats or on the floors of the cars to which they had been assigned.

Rail Journeys West

As early as the 1860s, settlers heading west could travel part of the way by rail, dodging flying sparks as they bounced along in crude passenger cars bound for the end of the line, St. Joseph, Missouri, the jumping-off place for many wagon trains. In 1869, with the driving of the gold spike that marked the completion of the nation's first transcontinental railroad, passengers traveling the Platte Valley route of the Union Pacific could reach San Francisco in less than four days—as opposed to the three to four months that journey took by wagon.

Since those riding "the cars" were allowed to check only 150 pounds of baggage for each full ticket purchased, women packing family belongings for a move west by rail operated under even tighter constraints than those who made the journey in wagons. In the 1880s some railroad companies offered special rates for "emigrant cars"—sparsely furnished boxcars that could be loaded with household goods, family members, and up to six head of cattle, plus grain and hay for the livestock.

Steamships and Ocean Voyages

This 1862 lithograph depicts one of the many steamers that made their way along the Missouri River to Fort Benton, Montana Territory, each spring during the emigration season. Thousands of settlers went west by riverboat, and thousands more—many of them forty-niners—made the long trip west by ocean, either by sailing all the way around Cape Horn or by braving the hardships of an isthmus crossing at Nicaragua or Panama.

While many Indians, blacks, and poor whites traveled west with whatever they could carry on their backs or on horses and mules, in 1863, Mary Barnard Aguirre, daughter of a Missouri merchant and wife of an aristocratic Mexican trader, emigrated to her new home in Las Cruces, New Mexico, in "comfortable carriages—costing $500 a piece" and boasting two facing seats "so that six people could be comfortably seated." Part of a large mule-drawn freight caravan of ten wagons—each drawn by "ten fine mules" and loaded with "10,000 lbs of freight"—the carriages themselves were designed with passenger comfort in mind and, according to Mary, were "built so they could be turned into beds at night just as a 'sleeper' seat is arranged now a days." There were boxes "under the back seat" for clothes and "pockets in the sides in the doors…[for] brushes, combs & looking glass."

Left: *This New Mexico settler prepares an evening meal on a wagon tailgate designed to serve as a cook table. Note the muddy wheels and the implements hanging along the sides of the wagon.*

Opposite, below: *A surrey laden with baggage and bedding conveys this early twentieth-century South Dakota emigrant to her new home.*

Below: *Though cooking in a kettle suspended over an open fire could be challenging, many women proved quite adept at preparing meals under adverse circumstances and went to great lengths to cook favorite dishes for their husbands and children.*

Cooking on the Trail

While Mary Barnard Aguirre was attended by numerous servants during her journey west, most of the women on the trail were obliged to handle all their normal household duties themselves—and often under the most trying of circumstances. "Camp life has no charm for me," Pamelia Fergus wrote her husband James at one point, though she admitted, "The children think it fun they want to eat all the time." A pioneer who made the crossing as a child noted in late adulthood, "Maybe it was hard for the grown folks, but for the children and young people it was just one long, perfect picnic."

As passages from Lillian Schlissel's *Women's Diaries of the Westward Journey* attest, women were hard-pressed to provide their families with three meals a day on this prolonged "picnic." Usually the food

Right: *With dogs play-ing at her heels and a toddler clinging to her skirts, the pioneer woman in this nineteenth-century engraving prepares supper, while her husband milks the cow and her two oldest children mind the baby.*

Opposite: *Unencum-bered by dress or family obligations, this 1907 Willow Creek Canyon, Colorado, camper flips her flapjacks with an abandon that would have puzzled, if not shocked, the pioneer women who traveled through the region fifty years earlier.*

was placed in a kettle suspended over the campfire by means of a pole laid across two forked sticks. Accidents and burned food were common, and emigrant Lodisa Frizzell complained that cooking out in the open "goes again the grane." Helen M. Carpenter, a honeymooner, shared Frizzell's sentiments. "Although there is not much to cook, the difficulty and inconvenience in doing it amounts to a great deal," Carpenter noted, "so by the time one has squatted around the fire and cooked bread and bacon, and made several dozen trips to and from the wagon—washed the dishes…and gotten things ready for an early breakfast, some of the others already have their night caps on—at any rate it is time to go to bed."

For those who had brought along a milk cow, there was always fresh milk for the children, and Pamelia Fergus reported that their "little cow from home" was giving "a nice lot of milk." After the evening's milk-ing, the remaining milk was usually placed in covered pails under the wagon, and in the morning the cream would be skimmed off and put into the tightly lidded churn to be turned into butter and buttermilk by the jolting of the wagon.

Eggs were scarce for families who did not bring along their own hens. Pamelia

Campfire Cooking

"It is very trying on the patience to cook and bake on a little green wood fire with the smoke blowing in your eyes so as to blind you, and shivering with cold so as to make the teeth chat-ter," noted eighteen-year-old Esther Hanna, a minister's wife.

Such difficulties notwithstanding, some women seemed to have had a knack for campfire cooking. Lydia Arnold Titus reported that she "fried home-cured ham or bacon with eggs" while she "boiled potatoes or roasted them in the hot ashes." Kitturah Belknap used a Dutch oven, a skillet, a coffeepot, and a teapot to create meals featuring salt-rising bread which she'd place "on the warm ground" to rise in the early evening.

Cecelia Adams reported that on a single Sunday in June she had "cooked beans and meat, stewed apples and baked suckeyes [pan-cakes]…besides making Dutch cheese." Charlotte Stearns Pengra noted an April day in which she "made griddle cakes, stewed berries and made tea for supper….made two loaves of bread stewed a pan of apples prepared potatoes and meat for breakfast."

Campfire Cuisine — Food from the Land

Well into the twentieth century, Native American lodges and tepees were built with a central vent to accommodate open-fire cooking. Some women boiled food by dropping red-hot stones into well-lined baskets. Others cooked in fire-resistant clay pots. As nomadic wanderings gave way to reservation living, heavy iron vessels were incorporated into traditional cooking practices.

The food eaten by herders and gatherers was obtained from the land. Women prepared and cooked buffalo and prairie chicken and also gathered and processed the berries, roots, and herbs that were a central part of tribal diets. According to Joy Yellowtail Toinetta, Crow Indians relied on natural sweeteners, harvesting honey from hollow trees and tapping box elders and cottonwoods for their sap. When cottonwood blossoms burst and flew, the sugar in the sap was at its peak, and couples went out in groups to scrape the wood and inner bark of the trees.

Fergus reported that farmers along the route had raised the price from seven cents to fifteen cents a dozen at the beginning of the emigration season. One diarist reported that fellow travelers had made a wedding cake with turtle eggs found along a riverbank. Catherine Haun noted that eggs were two and a half cents a dozen at Council Bluffs, Iowa, but "at our journey's end we paid $1 a piece, that is when we had the dollar." At Council Bluffs, chickens were worth eight to ten cents, but "when we reached Sacramento $10 was the ruling price and few to be had at that."

After the first week or so on the trail, when twigs and boughs from nearby woods could be gathered without too much difficulty, obtaining fuel for campfire cooking became a major concern for all travelers. In tall-grass country, women and children twisted prairie grass, slough grass, or hay into "cats," which burned well enough, provided the grasses were dry, though smoke was always a problem from such a fire. "We would collect grass and twist it into coils and burn it in our little stove…and we would pull grass the night before to get breakfast with next morning," wrote Martha Gay Masterson.

Once the trains had moved out onto the open prairie where trees and even grass were scarce or nonexistent, the pioneers were forced to rely upon buffalo dung— which some called *bois de vache*, meaning meadow muffins—for fuel. According to Mormon historian Stanley B. Kimball, few women took to the idea readily, as evidenced by lines from a popular trail song:

> *Look at her now with a pout on*
> *her lips*
> *As daintily with her fingertips*
> *She picks for the fire some buffalo*
> *chips.*

Eventually even the most squeamish gave in to the necessity of using the chips, especially since a bushel could be gathered in about a minute and generally "three bushels makes a good fire." Women and children were generally the gleaners, and for this purpose they carried large sacks as they walked alongside the wagons, gathering only enough for the evening and breakfast fires. Most agreed that when placed in shallow trenches over which the pots were suspended, the chips produced a hot, clear, virtually odorless flame. According to emigrant Helen Carpenter, "meadow muffins" had another beneficial use: Bringing one or two lighted chips into the wagon would soon smoke the mosquitoes out. "We can stand it longer than they can," Carpenter proudly noted.

In the last weeks of their journey, women who had earlier despised the buffalo chips found themselves wishing the animals had roamed farther west, since chips were far preferable to knotty hunks of pungent sagebrush, which burned too quickly to provide satisfactory fires for cooking. Along the southwestern trails, mesquite proved to be an excellent fuel. "This is the greatest country for firewood to have no timber growing on it that I ever saw in my life," one woman reported. "There is mesquit

brush growing everywhere. Some of it is dead and we dig the roots for firewood which makes the best coals of anything."

As Nancy Wilson Ross reported in *Westward the Women*, some emigrants found their experiences as trail cooks invigorating. A Mrs. Van Dusen, who migrated from Michigan to Oregon, used a "little round sheet-iron stove, about the size of a three-gallon bucket, with a little tea-kettle, a boiler and frying pan," where she cooked "with great ease and satisfaction." This stove was portable, so that she could cook while traveling, a luxury uncommon to most of the other women who crossed the plains. Indeed, Mrs. Van Dusen recalled with pleasure her "cosy little kitchen on wheels" and reported cleaning and cooking "a bird" while the wagon "moved along." The portable stove provided the family with warmth through the cold nights as well.

For homemakers whose cooking was done outside the wagons, outdoor conditions could make meal preparation doubly difficult. Mrs. Isaac Moore had just set dinner out for her family when a sandstorm hit the camp: She reported that "our most intimate friends could hardly have recognized us—so dirty were our faces. And our dinner! Who would have eaten

Below: Women and children on the overland trail gathered bois de vache, *or meadow* muffins, *as fuel for the evening's campfire. The chips produced a hot, clean flame that was virtually odorless, though smoldering remains gave off enough smoke to banish mosquitoes.*

Above: *"Deliver me from a thunderstorm on the plaines,"* Pamelia Fergus wrote during her 1864 emigration to Montana Territory. Horses, as well as passengers, were frightened by the winds, thunder, and lightning that accompanied such storms.

Right: The mud and muck that followed spring thaw made travel difficult for these Klondike women.

it? We could not tell what it consisted of, although before the storm it looked very tempting." In areas where mosquitoes were particularly thick, eating outdoors could be most uncomfortable, and one woman reported that her bread was "almost black" from the bodies of the mosquitoes that had found themselves mired in her rising dough.

Cooking on rainy days required a good deal of ingenuity and provoked many a show of temper from even the most patient of cooks. "You had better believe it [made] me cross when I had to get out and spat around in the mud to cook," complained Catherine Bell. Another woman reported that on such days there was "nothing to eat but crackers and raw bacon." Others refused to give up, some of them holding umbrellas over sputtering campfires, others digging holes for fires which were fed air through hollow reeds, the holes surrounded by rocks to support cookpots that sheltered the flames from the rain.

Left: Trekking through snow and ice was the norm for Klondike miners and packers moving through Chilkoot Pass early in the season. Treacherous at all times, the pass was doubly dangerous when wet spring snows loaded the slopes and heightened the possibility of slides. Over eighty people died in an avalanche in April of 1898.

Below: Dugouts in the snow provide shelter in a winter encampment in the Sierra Nevadas, not far from the end of the California Trail and near the site of the legendary Donner Party tragedy.

Weathering the Storms

Rain was an ever-present companion during the early spring months of most crossings, and Pamelia Fergus was especially frightened by the fierce storms, writing James, "Deliver me from a thunder storm of the plaines." After a particularly heavy midnight "storm on the Plat," she reported, "I will asure you we had eight cotten stufed comforteres wet through and not a dry rag to put on except those in our trunks every thing was wet in the wagon through a thick blanket and cover."

Amelia Stewart Knight reported on "a dreadful storm of rain and hail…and very sharp lighting" that killed two oxen. "The wind was so high I thought it would tear the wagons to pieces," she reported. "Nothing but the stoutest covers could stand it." And even those canvas tops that held against the wind were no insurance against the rain, which "beat into the wagons so that everything was wet in less than 2 hours the water was a foot deep all over our camp grounds." Since they had no tents pitched, "all had to crowd into the wagons and sleep in wet beds with their wet clothes on, without supper."

Washing wet and muddy bedding and clothing was no easy task, and many a diarist reported her distaste for the drudgery of doing laundry along the trail. Jane Augusta Gould noted in her diary that "at four P.M.

Below: Nineteenth-century magazine illustrations like this Harper's Weekly *etching fueled emigrants' fears of attacks by hostile Indians.*

I commenced and did a real large washing—spreading the clothes on the grass at sunset." Keeping babies in clean diapers posed special problems, and where water was scarce mothers often resorted to the practice of drying, scraping, and airing the diapers and reusing them without washing them at all until water was available and they could be boiled in a pot over a campfire. Often clothes boiled in a pot were then rinsed in a river or stream and hung on branches to dry.

Bedding Down for the Night

Dry bedding was essential to comfort and good health, for most of the emigrants slept in thin-walled tents that could be quite cold on rainy spring nights on the plains or frosty fall evenings in the mountains. The Fergus family kept their beds as dry as possible by putting down "Indian rubber sheets" before laying out their feather beds and quilts.

Body heat alone should have kept the occupants of the Fergus tent warm, for seven family members were crowded into "a tent that cost 34 dolars" and was "four

widths of ducking long [and] three wide"—little more than 9' x 12'. This arrangement, while adequate, was decidedly awkward, considering the lack of privacy enjoyed by the sleepers, two of whom were on their honeymoon. Mary Agnes, the eldest Fergus daughter, had married her Little Falls sweetheart, Robert Hamilton, just prior to the start of the journey west, and though Robert had hoped to provide his bride with a nuptial tent, ultimately the newlyweds joined Pamelia, the three other Fergus children, and Pamelia's brother, Thomas Dillin, in the family tent.

Travelers whose wagons were less heavily loaded than those of the Fergus family sometimes slept in the wagon boxes, while those who had brought along no tents and had no floor space to spare generally bedded down in the open air on quilts, feather ticks, or cornhusk mattresses.

Night Fears

Most families kept fires burning through the night to ward off intruders or wild animals—both large and small. Mary Moore

McLaughlin, who traveled by wagon to Iowa as a child, recalled the fear she felt in the evening, noting that, "as the twilight settled into darkness, the wolves came slinking around the camp; and while they howled we children snuggled closer together in our beds in the wagon box, begging father to build the fire higher."

Pamelia Fergus reported that she slept with a gun at her side, having heard reports that the Sioux and Crow were attacking wagon trains passing through their prime hunting grounds. Fergus, like most other Anglo pioneers, had only rumors and anecdotes on which to depend as she assessed the dangers she faced in the crossing. In actuality, there were relatively few Indian attacks on wagon trains, and Indians almost never attacked wagons that were pulled into a circle formation, preferring to take their chances with attacks on settlers whose wagons had broken off from the main train or whose stock had strayed too far from camp.

The Fergus family's one face-to-face encounter with Native Americans was more comic than tragic, according to Pamelia's daughter Luella, who reported that a small band of Indians wandered into their camp and "were looking around in our wagons, seeing what they could see" when Pamelia,

on impulse, "drop[ped] her [new false] teeth." Never having seen artificial teeth before, one woman

ran over to the other Indians, screaming and yelling, and they all took up the yell, leaving our camp in a hurry. A little later, they came back with a larger crowd and looked[ed] at mother…[thinking] that she was a great prophet or witch. They were afraid and yet they wanted to see if mother would do the same thing again. She would not, however, and it was not long before they all pulled up and left us.

Rebecca Ketcham, a young schoolteacher who rode across the plains on horseback, lacked the comfort and support of family members as she tried to overcome well-engrained fears of attacks by Indians. Riding on horseback with the men—and on a very slow horse at that—she once found herself lagging behind all the wagons and riders in the train. "Angry and hurt both," she was also "very much afraid," having been told "females were in great danger of being taken by the Indians because they think a high ransom will be paid for them."

Above: *Travelers on the Fisk Expedition of 1862 circled their wagons each evening as a safeguard against Indian attacks.*

Above: *Horatio Greenough's 1874 lithograph,* Daniel Boone Protects His Family, *not only perpetuated the myth of Boone as Indian-fighting frontiersman but also played into popular perceptions of woman as victim and Indian as savage. Artwork of this type was widespread in the 1870s, for clashes between soldiers and settlers and the Plains Indians were numerous from the close of the Civil War well into the 1880s.*

Ketcham's fears were probably well-founded, since separating oneself from the train did increase the chances of being attacked. Emigrant Catherine Haun tells of coming upon a "strange white woman with a little girl in her sheltering embrace." The woman and her five-year-old daughter—both of whom were "trembling with terror, tottering with hunger"—were the only survivors in a Wisconsin family of six who had dropped behind their train when the woman's husband and sister died of cholera. While their graves were being dug, Indians attacked the little party, killing or capturing everyone but the mother and daughter. Terrified, the two started back along the trail, hoping to meet up with an oncoming train. After three days of wandering—during which time their only food was a fish the woman caught with her hands and a squirrel she killed with a rock—they came upon the train in which Haun herself was riding. Though the woman's primary wish, at this point, was to go back home to Wisconsin, she was glad enough to find company and safety by join-

ing the train. Within a day they came across the wagon containing the bodies of the family members killed by cholera and Indians, and the tragedy was confirmed. Since her son's body was not among those found beside the wagons, the woman assumed that he had been carried off by the attackers. Though correct in that assumption, she was overjoyed a few weeks later to find that he was alive and well, having been traded to a family in another wagon train in exchange for a horse.

While relatively uncommon, such tragic clashes between Indians and whites added to the apprehensions of those making the journey west. One of the most infamous events, the Whitman massacre of 1847 in which missionaries Narcissa and Marcus Whitman and eleven others were slain by Cayuse Indians near Fort Walla Walla, roused fears for years thereafter. Disease and accidents actually claimed far more emigrant lives than did Native Americans— who themselves were all but annihilated by diseases introduced by soldiering or emigrating Anglos.

Illness and Accidents

Early trains were fairly fortunate in that there were not many epidemics on the excursions prior to the 1850s. Indeed, settlers coming from areas where malaria was a regular summertime threat generally enjoyed better health on the trail than did their friends and relatives back home in Iowa or Missouri. It is actually surprising that more general illness was not reported on these early trips, since waste disposal practices would hardly have met today's stringent standards. One fortunate woman enjoyed the luxury of a small "privy" in the back of her wagon, but there are no records as to how common such an arrangement was or of how the waste was disposed of. Most families used canvas-sheltered latrines in the evening when the train set up camp, but during the long days of constant motion, their only privacy might come from a circle of acquaintances or the relative shelter of the wagon itself.

Though it is likely the pioneers generally took care to set up their latrines at some distance from the springs or rivers that supplied their water, less was known about water-borne diseases at that time, and it is doubtful that adequate precautions against contamination of the water supply were taken by most parties.

All such problems aside, finding good drinking water was not always easy, especially in later years as larger trains traveling with assorted livestock taxed the rivers and springs along the way. Water became increasingly scarce once the wagons moved into present-day Wyoming. When the 1864 train in which Pamelia Fergus traveled turned north and headed through a valley between the Wind River Mountains and the Bighorns, they encountered creeks called "Poison Spring" and "Bad Water." Shortly thereafter, they entered a stretch of badlands containing no water at all, and the oxen became more and more irritable. By the time the train came upon a seep, the travelers were near panic, and though the wagonmaster ordered the men to dig down several feet and then ration out the water, with one bucket for each ox until all

had been watered, "someone violated this rule by giving his favorite oxen two buckets of water," thereby setting off a "free-for-all fist fight." Tensions eased when soon after the fight at the muddy watering hole the train arrived at Wind River, "a beautiful mountain stream with more than enough water for all."

For those trains that went on to California, passing through the Great Basin or the Humboldt Sink was particularly difficult, and Catherine Haun recalled that "the alkali dust of this territory was suffocating, irritating our throats and clouds of it often blinded us." Water was scarce, and Haun reported that "the mirages tantalized us; the water was unfit to drink or to use in any way; animals often perished or were so overcome by heat and exhaustion that they had to be abandoned."

Below: After days, or even weeks, of traveling through the badlands of Wyoming, South Dakota, or Utah, emigrants for whom safe drinking water was a constant concern found crystal-clear, tumbling waters a welcome sight.

Above: Amazed and delighted at the sight of "boiling springs" and geysers, some emigrants drank the mineral-rich waters as a tonic.

Right: The high vita-min C content of the prickly pear made this cactus an important component of both emigrant and Native American diets. The joints of young cacti were boiled so that the skin and needles could be easily removed and the soft interior could be fried. The prickly pear fruit itself could be eaten raw at the red-ripe stage.

Amelia Stewart Knight described a similar scene in the summer of 1853 in which they "had a great deal of trouble to keep the stock from drinking the poison or alkali water. It is almost sure to kill man or beast who drink it." Later Knight was amazed to come across "the boiling springs, a great curiosity. They bubble up out of the earth boiling hot. I have only to pour water on to my tea and it is made." However, there

was no cold water at all in the area, and the sulphurous stench and rising steam made her feel as if she were "in the bad place."

Many of the hot springs along the route west contained valuable minerals that could have improved the health of the travelers, just as the berries and prickly pear cactus that some of the travelers ate provided them with vitamin C, which was otherwise in scarce supply in the emigrant diet. Those women who had heard that scurvy was a major problem on the trail warded off the disease by including pickles, vinegar, and dried fruits on their lists of supplies. Catherine Haun's family relied on citric acid, which, when "mixed with sugar and water and a few drops of essence of lemon made a fine substitute for lemonade."

Other diseases were not so easily warded off, since by the time the symptoms of a contagious disease were recognized in one of the members of a train, others had usually been exposed to the carrier. With no antibiotics or other miracle drugs at hand, even a case of measles could end in death, especially where children were concerned. Measles epidemics were reported on several wagon trains, and Elisha Brooks, who made the crossing as a child, recalled "us children all lying in a row on the ground in our tent, somewhere in Iowa, stricken with the measles, while six inches of snow covered all the ground and the trees were brilliant with icicles."

Outbreaks of typhoid, whooping cough, smallpox, and chickenpox were also prevalent, and any of these diseases could prove to be deadly, given the wrong set of circumstances. Wet bedding, freezing winds, and rapid changes in temperature often resulted in colds which sometimes turned into pneumonia or "lung fever." Though most adult travelers managed to escape the childhood illnesses, dysentery—the "bloody flux"—hit almost every pioneer, and those who were weak or undernourished often died from it. Elizabeth Geer maintained that "no one should travel this road without medicine, for they are sure to have the summer complaint. Each family should have a box of physicking pills, a quart of castor oil, a quart of the best rum, and a large vial of peppermint essence."

Though their medicine kits were hardly adequate in view of some of the illnesses they encountered, women did take along whatever supplies they could gather. In addition to citric acid, Catherine Haun's family carried "quinine for malaria, hartshorn for snakebites…and opium and whiskey for everything else."

Ultimately, the medicine kits of the emigrants proved all but useless against cholera, the most deadly contagious disease to strike the trains. Partly because of the speed with which it spread and partly because of the poor sanitary practices of the travelers, cholera killed hundreds—some say thousands—of emigrants. From 1849 to 1854 cases were reported all over the country, and though some migrants had joined a train in hopes of escaping the disease, cholera followed them across the plains—where they died without benefit of physician or minister. In early June of 1852, Jane D. Kellogg noted that there was "an epidemic of cholera all along the Platte River. Think it was caused from drinking water from the holes dug by campers….All along the road up the Platte River was a grave yard; most any time of day you could see people burying their dead; some places five or six graves in a row, with board head signs with their names carved on them."

Judging from the entries in women's

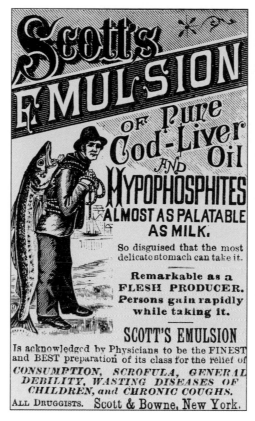

diaries of the period, counting the graves became a gruesome pastime among travelers who feared that their own families might soon face such a fate. While there are no complete records of the number of people who died in the early 1850s, some wagons lost two-thirds of their number, and one emigrant estimated fifteen hundred to two thousand grave sites along the trail west; another estimated five thousand. Those estimates might be low, since Stanley B. Kimball has estimated that of the seventy thousand Latter-day Saints who made the overland journey in wagons and handcarts between 1847 and the completion of the railroad in 1869, "at least six thousand died along the trail from exhaustion, exposure, disease, and lack of food."

Many of those who died were babies and children, and in at least one case, medicine rather than disease caused the death of a child. Lucy Henderson Deady's mother had brought along laudanum—tincture of opium—a fairly common item in nineteenth-century medicine kits. The bottle was suspended from a nail on the sideboard of the wagon, and Lucy's little sister, Salita,

Above: *Most westering families took along at least one or two of their favorite patent medicines. Though not available until the late 1870s, Lydia Pinkham's Vegetable Compound soon became the standard remedy for various "female complaints," largely due to the enthusiastic testimonials of prominent women, many of whom were leaders in the WCTU and likely unaware of the 18 percent alcohol content of this popular elixir.*

Right: *For Native Americans as well as the emigrants who were invading their lands, the loss of a loved one called for proper disposition of the body. These Oglala Sioux near Fort Laramie, Wyoming, have suspended the the remains of their fallen companion in the branches of a cottonwood tree.*

Below: *For little Elva Ingram, age four years, six months, the journey from Salem, Iowa, to Oregon ended near present-day Rock Springs, Wyoming, on June 28, 1852.*

drank the entire bottle. Complaining that she was sleepy, she then lay down on some bedding and was dead before the family realized what had happened to her. Her father made a coffin out of grooved walnut boards the family had been using as a table, and they buried the little girl "there by the roadside in the desert."

While the use of a wooden coffin should have been some guarantee against coyotes, many a traveler left a gravesite knowing that animals would soon dig up and desecrate the body of the loved one. Martha Gay Masterson and her siblings were probably typical of other children on the trail, in that they were both frightened and fascinated by the graves they found at each campsite:

If there were any graves near camp we would visit them and read the inscriptions. Sometimes we would see where wolves had dug into the graves after the dead bodies, and we saw long braids of golden hair telling of some young girl's burying place. We often saw human skulls bleached by sun and storms lying scattered around. The first ones we saw were shunned by us. We did not dare go near them. Later on, after becoming accustomed to seeing so many of them, we would pick them up and read the verses which some passerby had written on them, then perhaps add a line or two and set them up to attract someone else as they passed by.

Though there must have been adults who grew equally callous after observing so many graves along the trail, every burial site called up "a sad train of thought" for Jane Gould, who, after passing "a lonely nameless grave on the prairie," remarked, "it seems so sad to think of being buried and left alone in so wild a country with no one to plant a flower or shed a tear o'er one's grave." Katherine Dunlap recorded similar reactions after coming upon the grave of a child who died one month shy of her first birthday. "Oh, what a lonely, dark and desolate place to bury a sweet infant," she remarked, noting that the gravestone contained a note asking all who passed to repair the grave and that "it *was repaired* and a pen of logs built around it."

Though illness quite likely claimed the life of the infant whose grave Dunlap remarked upon, a goodly number of the children and adults died in accidents along the trail. An unattended child was vulnerable to all sorts of accidents—from rattlesnake bites to campfire burns. Often the difference between a comic and a tragic scene was quick action on the part of a bystander—as was the case when Arvazena Cooper's "dear little baby Belle" was rescued after falling into the water bucket while trying to help with the dishes.

Accidents in and around the wagons were quite common. Pamelia Fergus reported that five-year-old Frank Gravel "bar[e]ly escaped with his life" when the wagon rolled over him. And Maria Shrode noted that "Jennie fell out of the little wagon and both wheels ran over her arm and hand and one knee and bruised them considerably but did not brake any bones." Katherine Dunlap noted that "a little girl was jostled out of a wagon run over and killed." Children gathering berries or following a bird or butterfly could wander too far from the camp and get left behind—or worse. Dunlap reported that a pine board at the head of one trailside grave bore the inscription "Two children, killed by a stampede."

Birth on the Trail

Accidents and illness notwithstanding, except on those trains hit by epidemics of cholera, birth was almost as common a phenomenon as death. Indeed, Lucy Henderson Deady recalled that "Three days after my little sister…[Salita] drank the laudanum and died we stopped for a few hours, and my sister Olivia was born." Though hundreds of women were either pregnant when the journey began or became pregnant en route, few diarists made mention of pregnancy until the birth of a baby transformed an otherwise delicate topic into news that could be written without a blush. Though few wrote of the added difficulties pregnant women faced in stooping over a fire or jostling along a rutted roadbed, the discomforts of camp life were most certainly keenly felt by mothers-to-be.

Amelia Stewart Knight wrote page after page describing the "worst road that was ever made," a torturous section of trail that went "up and down…[over] very steep, rough and rocky hills, through mud holes, twisting and winding round stumps, logs and fallen trees" as she crossed the Cascade Mountains. After three days on this rugged trail, she noted: "I was sick all night and not able to get out of the wagon in the morning." Even then her diary contains no clue as to the nature of the "sickness,"

Below: Seated beside her wagon, a proud mother shows off her newborn to admiring family and friends. Births on the trail were almost as common as deaths, and names like Cora Montana, Salina Jane, and Gertrude Columbia served as permanent reminders of the site of a child's arrival.

though a subsequent passage notes, "A few days later my eighth child was born." There's no indication that the Knights delayed their journey in honor of the new arrival, since Amelia continues, "After this we picked up and ferried across the Columbia River [by] skiff, canoes and flatboat."

Moving on soon, if not immediately, after a baby's birth was apparently the norm, and Lucy Henderson Deady wrote that her mother had a most uncomfortable ride after the birth of baby Olivia. "The going was terribly rough," she noted, though "the men walked beside the wagons and tried to ease the wheels down into the rough places, but in spite of this it was a very rough ride for my mother and her new born babe."

Often the children in a family knew nothing about their mother's condition until the cry of a baby caught their attention. Martha Gay Masterson recalled being "awakened from a nervous sleep by the wailing of an infant. I asked mother whose baby was crying so. She said it was hers. I said not a word for some time, fearing I might have to welcome another brother. I already had nine brothers."

Equally surprised at the birth of a sibling was Oregon pioneer Annie Belshaw, who was having breakfast on the banks of the Columbia River "when some one told us that we had a little sister in the wagon with my mother." Whatever joy young Annie might have felt at news of the birth was soon lost, for little Gertrude Columbia "was only with [the family] two weeks."

While such scenes marred many crossings, historian Sandra Myres has observed that a survey of one hundred trail diaries revealed fourteen births and only three infant deaths. Her observations would suggest that childbirth on the trail, while less comfortable and convenient, was probably not profoundly more dangerous than childbirth at home, given the limitations of the obstetrical care of the era.

Keeping Spirits Up

Though weary from birthings and child-care and day-to-day chores, women on the trail obviously enjoyed moments of camaraderie in which they exchanged recipies and family stories while picking berries or gathering fuel with women from other wagons. According to Catherine Haun, though "high teas were not popular," tatting, knitting, crocheting, exchanging recipes, and "swapping food for the sake of variety" kept the women "in practice of feminine occupations and diversions." Maggie Hall's mother "knit all the way across" because "it took lots of knitting to keep [the family]… in stockings." Another woman was so adept at handiwork on the trail that she could knit or tat even while she drove the oxen.

It is doubtful whether such a tireless worker ever put down her handiwork—even on pleasant evenings in safe territory when the travelers lingered around the campfire for storytelling and readings. Jane Gould reported hearing "the merry notes of a violin" on an evening when "a general cheerfulness prevail[ed]." A priest who accompanied a Spanish expedition west reported that "a very bold widow…sang some verses which were not at all nice, applauded and cheered by all the crowd." Baseball games, debates, and spelling bees all helped pass the time and lift sagging

Courtship and Marriage

Though Lucy Henderson Deady, at fifteen, was not among those who married on the journey west, she reported that the single men in her train wondered "why a girl was not married if she was still single when she was sixteen."

Weddings on the trail were fairly common, especially on Mormon trains, where taking a second wife—or even a third—was considered cause for rejoicing among Mormon pilgrims bound for Zion. Edward Oliver, an Englishman whose wagon breakdown caused his family to winter over in Nebraska, was obliged to finish out his journey without the company of his wife, Sarah, when she announced that she and the children preferred to remain where they were until he got established out in Utah and sent for them. Edward agreed—but took Susana, the maid, along for company. Predictably, the two were married before they reached their destination.

When a Mormon encountered on the trail told the Gay family that he'd recently seen "a widow and her two daughters married to one man by the same ceremony," Martha Gay Masterson decided "that was too many sweethearts in one family."

spirits. And hunting and fishing were useful as well as enjoyable pastimes for men, women, and children.

Dances accompanied by fiddles or concertinas were not uncommon, and many an old melody was given new words that described events on the crossing. Mormon emigrants composed a number of hymns and songs that inspired the travelers and commemorated their courageous journey. Typical of the inspirational numbers was "The Handcart Song" recorded by Emma Batchelor Lee's biographer Juanita Brooks:

For some must push, and some must pull
as we go marching up the hill!
So merrily on our way we go,
until we reach the Valley, O!

Mormon trains and companies were also known for their lively dances, and place-names like Dance Hall Rock along the tortuous Hole-in-the-Rock Trail of southeastern Utah attest to their evening gaiety. These devout pilgrims also gave careful attention to sermons and scripture readings and to the observation of the sabbath.

Among secular trains, pausing for a day of rest on the sabbath was less common, though prepared or impromptu sermons were mentioned by a number of diarists who traveled in the presence of those inclined to celebrate the sabbath wherever they might be. Generally, even when a secular train did pause on a Sunday, its members weren't always unanimous as to how to spend the day of rest. More than one pious diarist reported being scandalized by women who gave more attention to doing their washing than to reading their Bibles during such layovers.

Women in the Saddle

Women who had been accustomed to limiting their activities to matters in their own sphere back home were often obliged on the trail to undertake tasks that would normally have been reserved for men. Mary Lyon's mother drove their wagon for a portion of every day, since her husband liked the exercise of walking along behind it. When the Lyon wagon was mired in deep mud, Mrs. Lyon mounted the family's horse and—with the baby in her arms and a young son seated behind her—helped guide the oxen out of the mud. Mollie Kelley, whose firebrand husband, Robert,

Above: For this Silver City, Idaho, family— and for others who made the journey west by wagon—picnics would forever be nostalgic reminders of meals shared around a campfire.

Right: *Left behind in Kansas when her husband headed for the goldfields, twenty-four-year-old Mollie Kelley grew tired of waiting, bought a wagon and a span of mules, loaded up her household goods, and headed for Montana Territory in the spring of 1864. Joining up with a train of eighty wagons, she drove her own team across the plains, with her two young daughters playing beside her on the seat or behind her in the wagon bed.*

had "hied him[self] away to that Rebel Paradise, Montana," in 1863, grew tired of waiting for her husband to come back to Kansas for her and decided to follow him west to Virginia City the next summer, driving a span of mules that pulled a wagon carrying her household goods, eight-year-old Kate, and three-year-old Nannie. Charlotte Stearns Pengra drove the family's wagon when her husband Byron came

Veteran of the Trail

Mary Wells Yates, a widow with thirteen children whose first overland emigration had been a sixteen-hundred-mile journey on horseback from Virginia to Missouri, had no trouble herding her "six shod cows" west, since those cows pulled the wagon she drove across the plains. Accompanied by her three oldest boys, she arrived in Virginia City in the summer of 1864, sold the cows at a profit, and soon thereafter went back for more of her children, whom she brought as far as Fort Benton, Montana Territory, on a Missouri River steamer, then took them the rest of the way to Virginia City in wagons.

On her next journey east, she drove a mule-drawn wagon both ways, bringing back a married daughter and her family—including the granddaughter born on the journey. An inveterate traveler whose expertise with a team was legendary, Mary, or "Granny," Yates, as she eventually came to be known, crossed the plains between Missouri and Montana thirteen times in all—usually driving her own wagon and often serving as guide and organizer for emigrant parties.

down with dysentery, driving the oxen until she was "quite outdone…[and] all used up."

Through eighteen miles of a blinding snowstorm, Kitturah Belknap drove the family's team so that her husband could herd the stock, reporting, "I thought my hands and nose would freeze. When I got to the fire it made me so sick I almost fainted." Catherine Haun reported that herding the stock, something she'd never done back east, was a "service …expected of us all—men and women alike."

Though not all women who made the overland journey showed enthusiasm for the traditionally masculine tasks they were sometimes obliged to undertake, their daughters often as not were fascinated by the challenge they posed. Mary Ellen Todd, a nine-year-old when her family headed west, had watched with fascination her father's cracking of the whip above the heads of the oxen who drew their wagon west and years later remembered:

> *Occasionally all along our journey, I had tried to crack that big whip. Now while out of the wagon, we kept trying until I was fairly successful. How my heart bounded a few days later, when I chanced to hear father say to mother, "Do you know that Mary Ellen is beginning to crack the whip?" Then how it fell again, when mother replied, "I am afraid it isn't a very ladylike thing for a girl to do."*

As the reaction of Mary Ellen Todd's mother indicates, gender distinctions were still important—if no longer sacred—to many women who made the journey west. Thus while most westering men paid heed to trail guides of the era that advised them to wear heavy boots, stout trousers, woolen shirts, waterproof jackets and coats, strong leather gloves and broad-brimmed hats, most of the women who went west traveled in the prescribed female garb of the day. Hooped skirts were particularly difficult to manage, and emigrant Helen Carpenter noted that she certainly "would not recommend [hoops] for this mode of traveling" since in climbing into and out of

a wagon "the wearer has less personal privacy than the Pawnee in his blanket." Most of those women who began the journey in hoops soon abandoned them, though without the hoops, their dresses dragged the ground, getting muddy or soaked with dew and often catching on twigs or briars. Carpenter's aunt and sister, bothered by high winds that "switched" their dresses around and made walking "precarious," pinned rocks along their hemlines—but found the wind so strong it banged the stones against their shins, causing Helen herself to declare that their "invention was not a success and so was never patented."

Other women forsook high fashion in favor of practicality, opting for cotton or linsey-woolsey dresses, ample aprons, and sunbonnets. But since any long-skirted garment, whether high-fashion or low, could be ignited by a campfire or caught under the wheels of a passing wagon, westering women clearly needed other options for day-to-day wear. In 1851, Amelia Bloomer's invention of a combination skirt and trouser outfit provided that option, and a few brave souls went west in bloomers—including the inventor herself, who emigrated to Ohio in 1853 and to Iowa two years later. Others traveled in similar outfits of their own devising, and emigrant Cora Agatz remarked upon a group of young women wearing "gymnasium costumes" made of grey wool. Outrageous as this seemed to some observers, Agatz noted that "when compared to the long, slovenly soiled cal-

ico gowns worn by the other women of the train, these simple costumes elicited many favorable remarks."

Practical or not, such outfits were eschewed by most women, particularly those who feared violating the biblical injunction "the woman shall not wear that which pertaineth unto a man." (Deuteronomy 22:5) That warning, plus social convention, kept most women in "ladylike" attire—even when the health and well-being of their families obliged them to undertake tasks that usually "pertain[ed] to a man."

For most pioneer women, the unorthodox tasks—and the unorthodox clothing—did not end the moment a wagon train reached its destination. Indeed, as these women helped unload the family's wagons and set about establishing a home in their new environment, most had every reason to be grateful for the lessons they'd learned during the long and arduous journey along the overland trail.

Above and below:
This whip-cracking Dakota Territory freighter might have found Amelia Bloomer's costume less cumbersome than her own long skirts. But how would bloomers have played in Deadwood?

A Home in the West

Pioneer Women Settling In

As more than one scholar of western history has suggested, for those nineteenth-century women who went west in covered wagons, life on the trail served as a fitting apprenticeship for life as a frontier wife. Certainly homemaking was somewhat easier in a stationary dwelling than it had been in a moving wagon, but the hard-learned lessons in "making do" came in handy as women settled into life in a strange and unfamiliar land. Many pioneers found that "home" in the West was quite different from the home they'd left behind in the East and, in most cases, ordinary domestic chores were made more difficult by the isolation in which the pioneers found themselves.

For most families, the first task attended to was finding or building a home, and since this had to be done quickly and efficiently, the pioneers generally used whatever materials they had on hand to fashion a shelter. Thus early settlers who'd moved west along the Ohio River fashioned their first cabins from logs salvaged from the rafts that had brought them to their new homesites. Similarly, for many who made the overland journey by wagon, the very vehicles that had carried them to their new home *became* that new home.

As historian Glenda Riley has noted, even if the wagon was not used as a home, it was generally put to some kind of use—perhaps as an extra sleeping area for a large family starting out with a small cabin, perhaps as a storage shed for clothing, food, or tools. Abbie Benedict used the covered wagon box as a root cellar in which to store her winter's supply of vegetables and cured meats.

If the women who journeyed west in the company of their husbands were sometimes shocked by the kinds of dwellings in which they were expected to begin homemaking, women like Emma Stratton Christie who followed homesteading or mining husbands west were often in for an even greater shock, since the descriptions they'd received from those husbands did

Opposite and below: *Where lumber was scarce, dismantling the wagons that had taken them west gave pioneers a good start toward building their homestead cabins.*

Above: *Settlers often used logs cut from trees on their own claims to build their first homes.*

Opposite, above: *An Arizona mother and daughter shape the green boughs that will frame their new home.*

Opposite, below: *Long, straight poles were used in the construction of this South Dakota tepee.*

not always fit the homes they saw when they got there. Though Emma Christie had been warned by her husband, David, that the new home he was building for them in Montana Territory was not quite the house she'd be leaving behind in Minnesota, it was probably just as well that the train was late pulling into Bozeman and that she spent her first night in the Territory in a hotel, for she was hardly prepared for the sight that met her eyes the next morning when David drove her and the six children up Bridger Canyon. Pointing with pride to the land he had chosen for his family, David admitted what Emma could plainly see: The "house" was little more than a pile of unpeeled logs and a stack of rough lumber. So the eight Christies spent their first Montana winter in a neighbor's claim shack, where Emma made the shanty's one room serve as the family's living quarters and prepared their meals in a lean-to kitchen.

Like the Christies, families who were fortunate enough to be moving into areas populated by relatives or friends often borrowed or shared quarters until they could build homes of their own. Recalling her own need for housing when she and her three oldest boys had first arrived in Virginia City, Mary Wells Yates later erected a series of rental cabins that came to be known as "Pilgrims Rest" and were a welcome sight to many a Montana immigrant.

Native American and Hispanic Dwellings

Anglo emigrants could have taken a lesson in home building from the Native American women in whose lands they were settling, for the various tribes designed their homes according to the materials available and the weather conditions that prevailed. On the Missouri frontier, Martha Gay and her parents observed Osage hunting village huts that "looked like inverted birds' nests." Made of "long green poles, sharpened at both ends…bent and stuck into the ground" so that the top ends crossed in the center to make a circle, these easily erected dwellings were covered with woven twigs, leaves, moss, and grass.

Emigrants moving to more northerly regions encountered dwellings of a different sort. Buffalo Bird Woman, a Hidatsa who grew up on the banks of the Missouri in Dakota Territory, described the lodges built by the women in her tribe:

> *My father's lodge, or, better, my mother's lodge—for an earth lodge belonged to the women who built it—was more carefully constructed than most winter lodges….Earth was heaped thick on the roof to keep in the warmth; and against the sloping walls without were leaned thorny rosebushes, to keep the dogs from climbing up and digging holes in the roof.*

According to historian Angie Debo, when more than three hundred Kickapoo Indians were forced to move from their homelands in Texas to Indian Territory (Oklahoma), they chose rich riverbottom land and constructed "an elegant and substantially built little village of bark houses" made of poles "bent to form an oval about sixteen feet long, twelve feet wide, and ten feet high, thickly covered with bark mats held in place with strips of bark and rawhide."

As historian Sandra Myres had noted, Spanish settlers moving to the Southwest sometimes took over Indian dwellings or built *jacales*, temporary shelters of brush, "pole houses" made of vertical limbs and chinked with moss and grass, or small adobes served by doors of "rawhide stretched on sticks." Sister Blandina Segale, of the Sisters of Charity of Cincinnati, described the adobe dwellings she found upon arriving at her mission site in Trinidad, Colorado, as being built of blocks made of "sunburnt mud" with mud floors and mud roofs built over rafters "as black as ebony."

Soddies and Tar-Paper Shacks

With timber hard to find, settlers in the Great American Desert—the central and northern plains—often built soddies of two-and-a-half-foot-long blocks cut from strips of previously untouched turf that were turned up and cut by a sod-breaking plow. One Iowa frontierswoman described such homes as "a hole dug down three feet or more in the ground and then a frame of whatever you could get made over that and sometimes only the sod (which was very tough) cut in squares and built up" with "no floors, or partitions, unless made of bed quilts," yet speculated that "there was more general happiness to be found in some of those shacks than was found in…more pretentious homes afterward."

According to historian Glenda Riley, soddies served Iowa settlers well, keeping them relatively cool in broiling summers and rel-

atively snug through harsh, snowy winters. They were cheap—with one settler claiming to have spent only $2.78 on his dwelling in 1870—though not much else could be said in their favor. The roofs of soddies tended to leak, and the dirt floors—which when dry could be scrubbed much as one would scrub a wooden floor—turned to muck when rain poured down from above, leading many settlers to put in rough board floors when lumber could be obtained.

Soddies, while not the most elegant of homes, provided more protection from the elements than did the tar-paper homesteader shacks used by emigrants to later frontiers. While South Dakota homesteading sisters Edith and Ida Mary Ammons felt fortunate to have been able to take up a claim being abandoned by a settler who'd already constructed a "home" on the property, Edith later recalled that

the tar-paper shack they found there was little more than a "none too substantial packing-box tossed haphazardly on the prairie which crept in at its very door." Crudely built of wide boards covered with black tar paper, the shack looked "as though the first wind would pick it up and send it flying through the air"—and those shacks that were not firmly anchored often did blow away or topple over, leaving their occupants and their contents to the mercy of the unceasing winds of the prairie.

The Ammons home, like most of the other tar-paper shacks constructed in the early part of the twentieth century, was the family's easiest means of meeting the government's demand that homesteaders live on their claims in dwellings at least ten feet by twelve feet in size. Economy, not comfort, was the primary concern of most of the settlers who tried their luck on this desolate frontier, and when drought drove all but the hardiest back to wherever they'd come from, the shacks they left behind represented no great loss.

On the plains and in states farther west, homesteading families with adult children who had claimed separate segments of land often favored tar-paper shacks for their relative portability, since dwellings were often moved from one claim to another in anticipation of a visit from Land Office inspectors. As Clark Shipman, a central Montana homesteader in the 1880s, demonstrated, even log cabins could be moved from claim to claim—if one built them on skids rather than on more solid foundations.

Above: Tar-paper shacks were an economical means of meeting government regulations stating that homesteaders must live on their claims in dwellings that were at least ten feet by twelve feet in size.

Opposite, above: Though dark and dreary, soddies such as this one afforded protection from biting winds and subzero temperatures.

Opposite, below: By the 1880s, these Nebraska pioneers had graduated to a spacious sod home with curtained, double-hung windows.

Above: *An African-American family in the dugout they built in 1889, soon after Oklahoma was designated a territory and opened to non-Indian settlers.*

Below: The Pioneer's Home on the Western Frontier—*an idealized picture by Currier and Ives, 1867.*

Turning a House into a Home

While nineteenth-century tradition referred to a man's home as his castle, most westering men were too intent upon plowing fields, staking mining claims, or scrambling to find day-labor jobs in temporarily booming economies to give much thought to the first dwellings into which they moved themselves and their families. Home was not, after all, the place in which they spent most of their waking hours.

In contrast, most of the wives who found themselves obliged to set up housekeeping in spartan log cabins with no doors or windows, mining shacks with dirt floors and canvas ceilings, flimsy tar-paper shacks, dark and desolate dugouts, or dusty brown soddies were confined within those dwellings around the clock—except for the hours they spent attending to outside chores related to their housekeeping duties.

Not surprisingly, some women gave in to despair the moment they saw their new "homes." Anna Shaw noted that her mother crossed the threshold of their new home on the Michigan frontier in silence and stood looking around at the dimly lit interior until "something within her seemed to give way, and she sank upon the ground." Others set about at once to improve their situation. Faced with a home which had "neither floor nor chimney" and whose wide cracks "admitted both draughts and vermin," Oregon settler Bethenia Owens-Adair recalled "gather[ing] grass and fern, mix[ing] them with mud" and filling the cracks, "thus shutting out the snakes and lizards."

Bertha Anderson, who went directly to a homestead in Glendive, Montana, upon leaving the ship that had brought her to this country from Denmark, moved into a "log house consisting of two rooms" that a relative had purchased for them for the sum of two hundred dollars. There were "cracks in the floor wide enough to stick a knife or fork through," and she had to tear up the flooring more than once to retrieve the precious tableware the children had pushed through the cracks.

Anderson was barely settled in that home when her husband and his brother decided they should move farther away from the river to a place where they could get "a full quarter section of land," which he expected to need if his dairy operation grew as anticipated. Since the most portable building on their old site was "a fairly good sized chicken house," the men decided "to move that first and to use that for [a] living house until the other one could be made ready." There was no floor, though Anderson says, "we didn't mind, as it was toward summer, and I had some old canvas and old carpets and gunnysacks. I stretched it on the ground and pegged it down as well as I could." Before she could get her furniture moved in, pack rats "dragged in at least a wheelbarrow load" of unidentified debris. "We cleaned them out as well as we could," Anderson reported, "and then we were at home."

By this time the family had acquired "one real bed" and a table from "some people leaving the country," paying for their purchases with some of Anderson's cheese. Barely twelve by twelve in size, this chicken-house home was "crowded quarters for five little children and three grown people." Bothered by the look and the smell of "the old gray logs that the chickens had so lately inhabited," Anderson "set to work again with old newspaper to cover them."

In a few short months the family was settled in the home they were to occupy for the next several years, having "fixed [it] up as well as a log house could be, except for the roof, which often leaked when we had heavy rains." Fortunately for the roof—if not for the grass in their fields—rains were fairly infrequent in that arid region, for every downpour was a housekeeping disaster since "the ceilings were made of muslin tacked up tight to look like plaster," and when the roof leaked "it was not only water which came through, but the muslin

would hang heavy with mud. Then it had to be taken down and washed and put up ready for the next rain."

Seeing this home as more permanent than her last, Anderson at first whitewashed the walls, then, when the family grew "more prosperous" she "got a figured cloth like calico and sewed it together width by width" then tacked it onto the walls "at the top, in the four corners and finally at the bottom." The front room had a single window, over which she hung "a cheese cloth curtain on which [she] had crocheted some lace."

Feeling that her babies deserved a better place to play than the rough plank floor, she spent most of one winter "sewing carpet rags," using "every available scrap" and

Above: *Turn-of-the-century Montana settler Carrie Dunn insulated the walls of her kitchen with newspaper.*

Below: *A sturdy swing hangs from the foremost log supporting the sod roof of this Custer County, Nebraska, dugout. Apparently the rich prairie soil has yielded a bumper crop of onions and squash, and the fresh-cut load of sod blocks in the wagon on the roof would suggest that remodeling or expansion is underway. The young woman in the suit and bonnet may well have been a teacher boarding with the family.*

even going to the dump to dig about for flour sacks, which she "dyed a dull brown in copper." Once the scraps had all been sewn, they were woven into carpets by a Mrs. Kemmis, a settler who had recently acquired a loom and had offered to weave rags into carpets for her neighbors. By spring the "little ones" were enjoying "rolling and playing" on the carpeted floor of the front room, and Anderson recalled "what a joy [it was] to have those rough, unplaned cottonwood boards covered." However,

The joy…lasted only a week, and then it started to rain, and after it had rained a whole day it began to leak through the roof. I felt so discouraged I didn't even care to go to bed, but finally common sense got the upper hand and I slept soundly. The girls woke me up by coming from their room wet as drowned rats. Their nighties were clinging to them, and they cried to get into our bed, but that was not any better. The ceil-

ing hung like a sack of mud. The poor carpet which was supposed to be striped, had now faded and the colors had gone, so that it was a dirty mess. I even forget if we went to our wet beds again, for sometimes it is a blessing to forget.

But rain is a blessing in a dry land, and Anderson added, "I do remember that when the sun came out and the rain had ceased, and the dirty carpet was put out on the fence to dry, we could not help but to be glad for the rain, since it would assure us of both hay and grain for the stock for the year."

All across the frontier, women like Bertha Anderson showed resilience and ingenuity as they sought to make less-than-ideal dwellings into comfortable homes. One Oklahoma settler "sewed sheets together & tacked [them] up to the joists as a ceiling." This same woman used "58 yards of new rag carpet" to insulate the outside walls of their drafty dwelling. Mary Hallock Foote, wife of a civil engineer, lined the walls of one of her first homes in the West

A Home in the West

with her husband's geological survey maps, much to the amusement of his colleagues, who thought it "peculiarly feminine" to display "old Silurian and the Tertiary deposits for the sake of their pretty colors."

By the early years of the twentieth century, the "tar paper homesteaders" of South Dakota had their choice of red or blue building paper for lining interior walls, and Edith Ammons noted that "we should all have frozen to death without it." There was an element of pride attached to one's choice of color for this "regulation shack lining," since "the red was a thinner, inferior quality and cost about three dollars a roll, while the heavy blue cost six." Since everyone was well aware of the grade and price of those two colors, "blue paper on the walls was as much a sign of class on the frontier as blue blood in Boston."

Frontier Furnishings

A home's furnishings were another indication of the relative wealth or poverty of its owners, with furnishings generally improving as the family prospered. Of course, the very wealthy had fine furnishings from the start—either shipping their heirloom tables, sideboards, beds, and pianos by ship, wagon, or rail or ordering elegant pieces once they had completed their homes and were ready to settle in.

In contrast, Bertha Anderson's first home was "entirely bare except for a little homemade table," though she soon found "a discarded stove and enough old boards lying around to nail together some kind of a bed for ourselves." For chairs they used a homemade bench for the children and improvised with "the ends of trees which were sawed off straight" for the adults.

Above: The ornate parlor furnishings of Mollie Byrne's State Street home in Helena, Montana, are reminiscent of those she chose for the parlors of the elegant houses she operated in the city's tenderloin district, where she was known as Belle Crafton before she made her bid for respectability.

Right: Anglo mothers concerned about devising a proper crib for baby would have done well to emulate their Native American neighbors, whose infants were laced into cradleboards. Consisting of a wooden frame and a pouch made of soft hides, the boards were always kept upright, whether hanging inside a tepee, leaning against a lodge covering, suspended from a tree limb, or strapped to a travois. Some boards were highly decorative, others plainer in style, and a baby's tribe could often be deduced from the trappings of the cradleboard in which it slept.

Those furnishings served them through their summer in the chickenhouse home, but by the time Anderson put down rag carpets in their new log home, she had also acquired "some second hand chairs, a dresser and even two rockers" and was relatively pleased with their situation: "We liked our home," she wrote in later years, "maybe better than some rich people like theirs."

Lizzie Sisk expressed similar sentiments—even though her first home had only "bunks to sleep in" and "stakes driven in the ground and rough boards placed on poles…fastened with pegs to the stakes" for a table. Her furnishings were not that different from those described by Waheenee, the Hidatsa Indian woman whose mother had built a fine earth lodge, around whose walls "stood the family beds, six of them, covered each with an old tent skin on a frame of poles." Indian and Anglo women knew the importance of recycling items that had become too worn to serve their original purposes.

Emigrants fortunate enough to arrive in wagons often brought furnishings from home, though in some cases the heaviest pieces—cookstoves and iron bedsteads—were lost when a family was forced to leave items along the trail in order to lighten the load for weary oxen no longer able to pull such weight through deep mud or up steep slopes. Even those who went west by water or rail tried to bring with them certain treasured heirlooms—such as the chest Bertha Anderson brought from Denmark. Though split beyond repair on its journey across the plains, the chest served the family well in its early years as Anderson noted, "I took the top with its curved lid and used it for a cradle for the baby…. The bottom I used for the clothes we did not wear every day."

A bed for baby was a priority item in most homes, and when Arizona ranchwife Sadie Martin had "nothing to use for a bassinet," she and her husband fashioned one from "a wooden canned goods box, cutting it low in front and at the foot, but leaving it high at the head and back." She lined the box, put in a pillow for a mattress, and set it on a chair by their bed, where "it answered the purpose very well." Little Brayton slept there until he was "big enough for a larger bed." As more and more families moved into California gold rush towns, carpenter William Hiller reported to his wife, Abiah, back home in New York, that though he had started out building homes and shops, newly arrived mothers were now keeping him busy with requests for cradles "to jog their babies in" and little wagons "to draw them in."

Utilities—Such as They Were

Even those families who were fortunate enough to be able to afford such items did not always enjoy running water. In the West, as in the East, the acquisition of indoor plumbing was dependent upon one's location and financial circumstance. As cities grew, water supply systems consisting of pipes and flumes that led from rivers or springs into various types of storage tanks made water less of a worry for urban dwellers, but for settlers in outlying regions obtaining water remained a primary concern.

Some rural families chose building sites near rivers or natural springs, but most eventually dug or drilled wells—though digging a well did not always mean finding good water. Families in arid regions often went through severe droughts in which rivers, streams, and aquifers dried up. Though eventually new technology and increased incomes allowed dryland farmers and ranchers to dig deeper and better wells, many started out with inadequate water supplies located some distance from their homes.

For a number of years, the Otto Dunlaps, who had come to South Dakota from an Iowa farm with a good water supply, had to haul water a half mile in two fifty-gallon barrels mounted on a stoneboat and dragged across the prairie by horses. The barrels were set outside the kitchen and protected from dirt and animals by two upturned washtubs. In the winter, snow could be melted to supplement the meager water supply, but as a rule the family did not rinse their dishes and two or three people bathed in each tubful of water—after which the bathwater was used to wash floors or launder heavy overalls. In the drought years that followed, several rivers in the area dried up, leaving settlers to take their water from sinkholes, boil it, and store it in jars.

Above: *Pumping water was a daily chore on the Pope homestead in Slope County, North Dakota. With drought a constant threat, the sound of water in the pail was music to the ears of most farm women.*

Right: *Having driven the wagon to the nearest waterhole, this young plainswoman is filling the barrel brimful of the precious liquid.*

Even rural settlers with adequate water supplies relied upon outhouses for disposal of human household wastes. Though relatively few letters, diaries, and memoirs make any mention of this delicate subject, historian Glenda Riley found that one Iowa homesteader "br[oke] with convention" by noting that "outhouse accommodations were the thick brush or a couple of fallen tree-trunks; one for men, one for women." More advanced homes might have privies or outhouses made of sod or slabs.

In describing an elegant Victorian home in a Colorado silver town, historian Elliott West writes that the elaborate dwelling boasted "a nine-seater outhouse with a servants' entrance." In inclement weather, the owners of such homes could avoid going outside by using porcelain chamber pots, and Emily French, a Colorado divorcée who had taken great pride in building a home for herself and her children, writes of "carr[ying] out the slops" for one of the well-to-do families for which she worked. Though they had no servants to empty them, families of lesser means often had a chamber pot or two—either a purchased enamel vessel or an old lard tin.

In sizable towns and cities, "honeywagons" regularly picked up "slops" from in front of doorways and disposed of them in nearby rivers and streams. During Denver's early boom days, the wagons dumped their contents into the South Platte River—as did the garbage wagons—reducing the river's flow and increasing its bacterial contamination. Even with the introduction of indoor plumbing, most cities continued to dump human waste into the nearest river.

Adequate lighting was often a problem in frontier homes, many of which had few, if any, windows. A woman who moved to an isolated homestead in the West might find herself sewing and cooking by candlelight, though her eastern home had been illuminated by gaslight. The saucer lamp was one of the most popular lighting appliances on the Iowa frontier, and Margaret Archer Murray recalled making such lamps by dipping a twisted-rag wick in lard, then placing one end of the rag in a shallow dish filled with melted lard—"then it was ready to light." Mary Ellis reported that her family fueled similar lamps with "coons oil," rather than lard. Despite the inadequacy of such lighting, Murray noted that her mother "made all our cloths by hand knit all our stockings and mittens by lamp light."

Other families dipped or molded candles or purchased them at trading posts or stores, and as kerosene and other fuels became more easily obtainable, families gradually turned to more conventional lamps and lanterns. Thus Sarah Yesler lighted her first home in Seattle with lanterns and candles, but in the early 1870s her husband Henry—

who had also started that settlement's first water system, a pipeline of eight- to twelve-foot logs bored to four-inch diameters and joined together along a trestle—was a partner in the enterprise that lit up the city's homes with gaslight.

Protection from the Elements

Once frontier women had made their homes as comfortable as possible and had done their best to solve water, waste disposal, and lighting problems, they were still faced with the task of protecting themselves from the elements. Pamelia Fergus, left on

Above: *Rainwater collected in the barrel at the corner of this house was used for drinking, bathing, and laundry.*

Left: *Their new well, complete with windlass and pulley, was a source of pride for this Nebraska family.*

Above: With her mountain home all but buried in snow, Colorado settler Lorna Page cures cabin fever by hitching her dog to a sled and enjoying a bit of outdoor recreation.

her own to manage family affairs in the frontier town of Little Falls, Minnesota, during her husband James's sojourn at Pikes Peak in 1860, reported that she had followed his advice and asked the family's hired man, John Currie, to help her plaster the cracks in the kitchen walls and bank the house with mounds of dirt against the winter's cold.

Over fifty years later, South Dakota tar-paper homesteaders winterized their houses in similar fashion, using sod and a mixture of straw and manure to help weigh down the structure, lining their walls with whatever paper or cloth they could spare, though the porous sides of those dwellings did little more than filter out some of the snow carried on fierce blizzard winds. Inside such a shanty, one could generally manage to keep warm enough to survive—provided there was enough wood to keep the fire going. Outside, people and animals froze to death in temperatures so low one homesteader reported the mercury had disappeared into the ball and would read no lower than forty below.

With the temperature dropping, Edith Ammons hitched their horse to the buggy and started toward the school in which her sister Ida Mary taught. As the two returned to their tar-paper home, they saw in the distance a blizzard "coming like white smoke." Realizing that the horse's slow pace was no match for the quickly moving storm, they hopped out of the buggy and raced for the house, leaving the horse to find his way to the shed without their help. Later Edith recalled that "cowering in that tiny shack…the wind screaming across the Plains, hurling the snow against that frail protection, defenseless against the elemental fury of the storm was like drifting in a small boat at sea, tossed and buffeted by waves, each one threatening to engulf you."

Summer heat could be equally dangerous in such a home, since temperatures climbed to the high nineties and beyond and the black buildings absorbed the sun and baked their occupants. At such times the ever-present winds that seeped through the porous walls were more than welcome, though those same hot winds, which Marjorie Clark maintained could "actually [blow] the feathers off the chickens' backs," could also fan the slightest spark—from a steam thresher, a cookstove, or a careless smoker—into a roaring conflagration that engulfed the dry grasses and all else that lay in its path. Kansas settler Lillian Smith recalled many a night when her mother

stayed up all night watching the red glare of the prairie fires in more than one direction, in fear and trembling that they might come swooping down upon us asleep in our little log cabin....As soon as she would see the fire getting close, away we would go with our buckets of water and rags tied to hoes, rakes and sticks, wet them and set a back fire to meet the monster coming, so when it reached our line we would stand still and wait until we knew it had passed us by for that time.

Torrential rains, though always welcome in dry western climates, sometimes caused flooding that destroyed or damaged homes and outbuildings. Particularly across the Great Plains, storms often spawned tornados. Annie Green, a settler who had gone to Greeley, Colorado, in a homesteading experiment promoted by the noted newspaper editor who gave his name to the town, was not too worried when the wind picked up one afternoon, since she'd heard old settlers say they'd never heard of tornados or whirlwinds out in Colorado. Suddenly "an approaching roaring, similar to that of the [railroad] cars close by," heralded "instant darkness" that sent her children running to her arms, screaming in alarm. Seconds later, she "sank to the floor," where she remained until "the alarm of fire" roused her from her faint. She rushed to the window in time to see "a new house...lifted from its foundation and hurled to the ground" and another lifted up and slammed into a third dwelling. "The air was literally filled with paper roofs, pieces of timber, clothes baskets, and men's hats." Paralyzed by fear, she "breath[ed] a

Above: *While families on the open plains lived in perpetual fear of prairie wildfires, forest fires posed equal hazards for settlers living in wooded areas.*

Left: *Heavy rains in Dakota Territory in the spring of 1881 sent the Missouri over its banks, flooding most of the homes in Vermillion.*

Opposite, above: In this nineteenth-century woodcut, a pioneer mother fends off a fierce grizzly with an axe.

Opposite, below: Part of a constant stream of anti-Indian propaganda, this broadside compares "merciless Savages…fatally engaged in the work of death" to the cholera plague that was sweeping the nation.

Right: For settlers unlucky enough to build their homes near—or over—rattlesnake dens, encounters with reptiles this size were all too frequent. South Dakota homesteader Bess Corey reported routinely killing five or six snakes anytime she walked across her claim.

prayer of thankfulness to [her] Protector," for the tornado had passed through her yard, yet left her home intact.

Other settlers experienced floods that destroyed their homes and endangered their lives. A Mrs. Van Court, who lived in the Santa Cruz Mountains of coastal California, recalled seeing San Gregorio Creek, which could normally be waded across, rise so quickly and spread so far after a torrential rain that "trees two hundred feet high went down that stream like pipe stems, [and] every thing they struck had to go with them." Mrs. Van Court's "next neighbor towards the ocean lost every thing they had but their lives," and her own family was cut off from the stores in nearby Pescadero for nearly a month.

Warding Off Insects and Animals

Flooding often set off a plague of mosquitoes, though those pesky insects—along with flies and gnats—annoyed settlers in drier climates as well. With no screens to

keep the insects out of her Iowa home, Matilda Peitzke Paul recalled that her family made a smudge of dried buffalo chips to discourage the mosquitoes and used "a little limb, thick with leaves, to keep…[the flies] off food while we ate."

Pesky as they were, flies were welcome visitors compared to the rattlesnakes that paid calls on many a settler in the open plains. South Dakota homesteader and schoolteacher Bess Corey estimated that "thousands" of rattlers lived in a den near her home, and since she routinely killed five or six snakes anytime she walked across her claim, she dared not go outside at night for fear of stepping on a snake. When neighboring ranchers finally dynamited the den in hopes of eliminating the problem, Corey reported that they "got 300 all together and guessed that 3000 got away."

As Arizona schoolteacher Angie Mitchell soon discovered, skunks as well as snakes were prone to invade the homes of early settlers. Against the advice of her fiancé, who questioned her *craziness* in wanting to go to such an out of the way place," Mitchell had accepted a post at Tonto School, west of Prescott. Boarding at a remote ranch, she found herself in the company of a number of women but very few men, since the men generally worked away from home. Late one night a skunk got into the house and Mitchell reported that "Mrs. Harer sprang up & called me and run outside after the skunk & tumbled him over but in a second he jumped & ran into a catclaw bush." As the outraged woman chased the skunk with a pole, "striking violent blows" but damaging only the ground, the younger women inside barricaded the door to keep the animal out of the house. Finally "his skunkship crawled into a sage brush and… [we] demolished him with poles & met with no more accidents except that we got a liberal dose of perfume." It was late October, and the Arizona creek in which they washed themselves was "cold enough to nearly freeze one." Having "got rid of the smell as well as [they] could," the women "got on clean night gowns…and carried the old ones on sticks a little way down the creek & buried them in the sand" before going back to bed.

As if skunks weren't company enough for this young teacher, that same fall she was "wakened from sleep sometime after midnight by a tremendous purring noise," at which point she saw "the mouth & nose of some animal" poking through "a chink some 3 inches wide" where a pole had been taken out to let in the evening air. At her scream, the face withdrew and "a big, furry paw" came through the crack, "evidently trying to catch hold of [her]." Her second scream was "echoed from outside by a long, peculiar wail like a woman or child crying," at which point she knew her visitor was a "'cougar'—or 'mountain lion' or 'California lion.'" Once the intrepid young woman had made sure the doors and windows were secure, she drifted off to sleep again, knowing the cat would be gone with the dawn.

Ironically, Colorado homesteader Annie Green had to defend her home from stampeding stock rather than mountain lions. With her husband too ill and "feeble to attend to anything," she woke up early one morning to find fifty head of open range cattle feeding on their forty acres of oats. Taking with her "the broom stick, which is termed the woman's weapon," she set out in pursuit of the cattle, but "gave out before I had got halfway across the field."

Neighborhood Dynamics

As if roaming or stampeding animals weren't enough to put up with, frontierswomen were often bothered by unannounced visits from men who were looking for food or work and did not always behave as gentlemen when they found a woman alone on an isolated ranch. Kate Aplington, an 1880s emigrant to the Kansas frontier, kept "a cup of cayenne pepper and a cornknife within reach" as a safeguard against any "vicious-minded stragglers," figuring she could "make things hot and interesting for a tramp!"

Of particular concern to Sister Blandina Segale were the cowboys, of whom she'd heard many unsavory stories. En route to her mission in the West, she was horrified

when the stage in which she was riding stopped somewhere in the Colorado darkness and the driver's lantern revealed "a tall, lanky…man, wearing a broad brimmed hat" and carrying a buffalo robe. Settling himself on the bench beside her, the man held out the robe to the good sister and asked her if she'd like to share part of his "kiver." Before she could protest, he'd plopped half the robe across her lap. "The driver closed the door," she wrote to the nuns back home, "and we were in utter darkness."

By descriptions I had read I knew he was a cowboy! With crushing vividness—"No virtuous woman is safe near a cowboy" came to me. I made an act of contrition—concentrated my thoughts on the presence of

God—thought of the Archbishop's blessing, "Angels guard your steps," and moved to such position as would put my heart in range with his revolver. I expected he would speak—I answer—he fire.

Instead, the cowboy asked, "What kind of lady be you?" to which Sister Blandina stammered, "A Sister of Charity."

"Whose sister?" came his puzzled response, and with that exchange began a long conversation in which the sister discovered that the young man had run away from home six years ago and hadn't written a word to his mother since. Before their ride was over, the cowboy had promised the nun that he would pen a letter to his mother

just "as soon as [he got] off th[e] stage." Bidding him farewell at the next stop, Sister Blandina continued on to her destination city of Trinidad with a new appreciation of the creature called the cowboy.

Judging from the sentiments expressed in hundreds of memoirs, diaries, and letters written by pioneer women, Indians, rather than cowboys, were the people most feared, though it is also true that in expressing fears about native peoples they were acting out of cultural expectations. Hardly a letter came from the East that did not contain questions and concerns about the "savages" in the West, yet except in those areas where Anglos and Indians were feuding over treaty violations or involved in ongoing conflicts stemming from previous grievances, encounters between Indians and pioneer women were, as a rule, relatively peaceful, with both races expressing more curiosity about, than hostility toward, the other.

When an Indian slipped, unobserved, into the kitchen of Bertha Anderson's home in Montana Territory, she was frightened at first but "quickly collected [her] wits and began spreading bread and butter with meat and cheese and set it on the table." By the time she had fed him "a whole loaf of bread," the man "began to speak, if we can call it so." Holding up three fingers he "said just one word, 'Papoose.'" Feeling "relieved and proud, too," Anderson held up five fingers and said, "Papoose." The Indian held up two fingers and said, "Guns," to which Anderson, who had no firearms, shook her head. When he held up several fingers and said "Ponies," she reciprocated, pleased that "there [also] I could beat him. The next time it was 'Dogs,' but we did not have any, so he had the best of me there." When their "conversation…which consisted in just four words, with never a smile or a muscle moving in [the Indian's] face" was over, the man departed "as silently as he had come."

With verbal communication limited by language differences, women like Bertha Anderson learned to pay attention to the dress and body language of the Indians who

came to their doorstep. From her earliest interactions with the natives in and around the area in southwestern Oregon where her family had settled, Martha Gay Masterson determined that Indians dressed in war paint were not to be trusted, while those in ordinary dress were generally friendly and would leave without causing trouble. She learned as well that such distinctions did not necessarily apply to Indians who had been drinking, since the actions of drunk Indians, like those of drunk Anglos, were apt to be unpredictable.

Most women who managed to analyze the dynamics of an encounter with Indians survived that encounter and learned from it. Nonetheless, since there was always a chance that one could be wrong about a stranger's intentions, even women like Mary Sheehan Ronan, who, as the wife of a federally appointed Indian agent, was accustomed to frequent encounters with Native Americans, were not immune to fear. One morning during her early days on the agency Ronan was sitting on her porch, drying her hair, "which was heavy and wavy and hung below [her] knees." Suddenly Arlee, chief of the Salish, came up the steps and asked for her husband. Rising, Ronan

shook her hair back from her face and started into the house to find him.

I heard a moccasined tread behind me and felt my hair gathered by a hand at the nape of my neck. I was terror-stricken. There flashed into my mind childish fears I had had when trekking across the plains and the awful tales of scalpings related by emigrants by campfires at night. Fortunately, I did not have time to cry out or to show my fear in any way, for quickly I felt a second hand below the first, and so hand below hand the length of my hair. While the measuring was in progress Baptiste [Baptiste Marengo, an interpreter] spoke, saying that the Indians liked long hair, that Arlee had never seen any so long as mine and that he wanted to tell the tribe how many hands long it was.

If some women were fearful, others could be considered so bold as to be foolhardy. When Lydia Low of Washington Territory caught "a half-naked Indian" in the act of stealing a ham hanging from the rafters of her kitchen, she simply snatched up the

Above: *Etchings and woodcuts depicting settlers defending their homes against Indian attack were widely published in nineteenth-century newspapers and magazines, keeping families back east in constant fear for the safety of their loved ones out west.*

wooden spoon from the kettle of corn meal mush she'd been stirring and "applied it with direction and vigor to the Indian's bare behind," after which he "did not linger"— and dropped the ham as he fled.

It seems likely that Low, like many other Anglos, viewed all natives as thieves and treated them accordingly—probably without realizing that most natives likely had ample reason to hold similar views about the Anglos who had invaded their land and slaughtered the buffalo that were crucial to their survival. Pretty-Shield, a Crow woman, recalled, "my heart fell down when I began to see dead buffalo scattered all over our beautiful country, killed and skinned, and left to rot by white men, many, many hundred[s] of buffalo." Though Pretty-Shield had every reason to feel antagonistic toward white settlers, she maintained that she had never let herself "hate the whiteman," since she "knew that this would only make things worse for [her]." She, like other Indian women, learned the advantages of making friends with the invaders.

Thus, though there were some seemingly unprovoked attacks by natives, most hostile encounters were triggered by the mounting frustration felt by Indians who were rapidly losing their lands and their livelihood. Nevertheless, when word came that Native American warriors were attacking homes and villages, most settlers thought little and cared less about the reasons for an uprising, and word of the deaths of citizens or soldiers tended to arouse racial prejudice—as well as fear—in otherwise fair-minded people.

Ironically, Indian families were often equally fearful of whites. Sarah Winnemucca Hopkins, a member of the Paiute tribe, recalled a morning when her family was terrified "to hear some white people coming. Every one ran as best they could.... My aunt overtook us, and she said to my mother: 'Let us bury our girls, or we shall all be killed....' So they went to work and buried us, and told us if we heard any noise not to cry out, for if we did they would surely kill us...so our mothers buried me

and my cousin, planted sage bushes over our faces to keep the sun from burning them." The reactions of these Paiute women are understandable, since the kidnapping and raping of Indian women and girls was common practice on every American frontier, although until very recently most historians have given more emphasis to Indian attacks on white women.

According to Montana pioneer Mary Ronan, relations between Anglos and Indians at the agency on which she lived improved so drastically over the years that in her own house "no door or window was ever locked" out of fear of Indians—no small change in attitude for a woman who had crossed the plains hearing "the awful tales of scalpings related by emigrants by campfires at night" and who had once been terrified that she herself was about to be scalped.

Upward Mobility—Frontier Style
Though Mary Ronan had begun her life in the West in a crude miner's cabin, she even-

tually came to enjoy a relatively spacious home at the agency. Indeed, her memoirs note that Peter Ronan worked out "a system of waterworks" in which cold water was routed "through the milkhouse" and then "piped into the kitchen sink," thus providing Mary with the coveted "running water" that was the dream of many a pioneer woman. Furthermore, "a bathroom with a tin tub was improvised in a small room off the kitchen" and though hot water for the tub had to be "carried in pails from the large tank attached to the kitchen stove and emptied into the tub" and cold water had to be carried "in pails from the sink," she noted with some pride that "the water could be drained out through a rubber tube into a narrow irrigating ditch, a truly great convenience."

Mary Ronan had waited a long time for the "truly great convenience" of that tub, but her patience and fortitude were eventually rewarded. As another Montana pioneer, Bertha Anderson, once observed, "try[ing] again" was very much a part of

Above: *Philbrook, Montana, ranchwoman Ruby Goodell places clothes in a gas-powered washing machine driven by an elaborate set of pulleys rigged up by Homer Goodell.*

Opposite: *Paiute tribeswoman Sarah Winnemucca Hopkins wrote of her mother's terror at the approach of "some white people." Such fears were understandable, since kidnapping and raping of Indian women and girls was common practice.*

Above: *After the Valier Irrigation Project brought relative prosperity to the Wolverton farm in Pondera County, Montana, the family enlarged their home and constructed new outbuildings.*

Opposite: *Added in the early 1880s, the frame building on the right is the latest component of a fairly spacious ranch home that began as a small log cabin and grew with the fortunes of its owners.*

the experience of every pioneer woman, and trying long enough and hard enough to establish a comfortable home in the West was not without its rewards. Over and over again one reads about families who started out in dugouts and soddies and log cabins and ended up in fine homes that boasted not one but many "great convenience[s]," homes that gave testimony, to some extent, to the success of their pioneering enterprise.

Emma Christie's months in that one-room claim shanty up Bridger Canyon ended with a move into the "16 x 20" home "with a good high chamber in it" that David had promised her. That home, like the homes of many settlers, was gradually added on to, then finally abandoned entirely as the Christies celebrated the dawn of the new century by moving into a newly constructed two-story house with plenty of room for the six children who'd accompanied Emma on the railway car that had brought her to Montana and the three additional children born after her emigration.

Although the acquisition of a fine house with modern conveniences and ample fur-

nishings said something about the relative success of a couple's pioneering enterprise, Bertha Anderson maintained that "the best proof that all was well was the flock of healthy and sturdy youngsters we had around us." Her attitude is hardly surprising since, with a few notable exceptions, human relationships, rather than material wealth, were the primary concerns of most pioneer women—from Sister Blandina who gave her life to working to better the lives of the people of Trinidad, Colorado, to Seattle pioneer Sarah Yesler whose husband, friends, and many social causes were far more important to her than the elegant mansion her husband Henry erected in her honor.

Yesler Mansion eventually burned to the ground, but the work Sarah Yesler did to improve the lives of the citizens of Seattle lives on. Thus, in the end, the homes of pioneer women are of far less importance than the loving and the living that went on inside those homes—from the everyday activities that sustained family life to those special events that added richness and variety to an often difficult existence.

A Home in the West

Behind Closed Doors

Pioneer Women and Family Dynamics

As historian Lillian Schlissel noted in *Far from Home*, "In our national passion for frontiers, we have not considered very much how frontiers affected family life," despite the fact that in "three hundred years of American migrations, families have been routinely 'dis-assembled.'" The impact of this "dis-assembly" was ongoing, as evidenced by Annie Green's recollection of the anguish she felt during a Sunday afternoon in Greeley, Colorado, on which she was writing letters to relatives back home for whom her heart "panted continually." She had finished up the third letter in which she had used the phrase "until we should meet again" when the word "*never, never,* sounded in my ear, and penetrated my aching heart with an arrow, the effect of which I feel to this day."

Clearly, as Schlissel noted, "a family on an American frontier—wherever that frontier might be—was a family separated from some part of itself," a family longing to reconnect with those left behind through letters, through memory, through photographs—"anything out of which to weave continuity over the distances and the separations." Many sought that continuity by attempting to pattern their lives in the West after their lives in the East, though as California mining pioneer Louisa A. K. S. Clappe—later known as Dame Shirley—observed in an 1851 letter to her sister Molly, this was not always easy "in a place where there are no newspapers, no churches, lectures, concerts or theaters; no fresh books, no shopping, calling nor gossiping little tea-drinkings; no parties, no balls, no picnics, no *tableaux*, no charades…no promenades, no rides nor drives…no *nothing*."

Given these circumstances, and the fact that women on the frontier were operating without the direct assistance of the mothers and grandmothers who would normally have helped them establish and carry out family and community traditions, it is little wonder that more than one well-intentioned pioneer woman faltered in her attempts to

Opposite: *A rare glimpse at the lighter side of frontier living.*

Below: *Reading a long-awaited letter from the East.*

71

Above: *In contrast to earlier days when pioneer couples were obliged to stand before a justice of the peace to be wed, by 1872 marriages in Lane County, Oregon, could be carried out with all due ceremony and with the blessings of church and state.*

Clashing Courtship Customs

Most were, in fact, so busy attempting to establish their own brand of civilization that they failed to realize that the Native American and Hispanic women upon whose lands they were settling were operating out of well-established customs and rituals of their own. For example, many women coming west for the first time were particularly shocked to find that some Native American and Hispanic cultures had different ideas about the propriety of living with men to whom they were not formally married. As historian Sylvia Van Kirk noted, intermarriage between incoming traders or explorers and Indian women was fairly common in this country's early years. Though such unions were not always formalized according to the custom of the eastern seaboard colonies, marriage *à la façon du pays*—or according to the custom of the country—was honored and respected by Indians and Anglos alike. Many such unions were key factors in establishing and maintaining Indian-Anglo ties, and many couples united under such circumstances—including Sacajawea and Charbonneau of the Lewis and Clark Expedition—went on to enjoy long and fruitful relationships.

Marriage *à la façon du pays* was also fairly common in frontier towns where Anglo women were scarce and incoming laborers sought out Native American women as housekeepers and companions—only to abandon them as the settlement expanded and white wives became available. When Pamelia Fergus of Little Falls, Minnesota, discovered that Odishquaw Sloan, an Indian woman, had been deserted by John "Pewter-Eyed" Sloan, the father of two of her three children, Fergus hired the woman as her housekeeper, gave her food for her children, and—despite opposition and threats from the family of Sloan's Anglo wife—persuaded her husband James, who was Sloan's employer, to require the man to provide his former family with household goods and a living allowance of ten dollars a month.

do so. While failure to live up to the expectations of one's mother or grandmother must have been frustrating to westering women, at least that failure did not carry such a harsh penalty as it might have carried back East. There those august figures were on the scene to observe and perhaps comment upon one's day-to-day failings as homemaker, wife, and mother or as a single woman seeking fulfillment outside the bounds of matrimony—or even outside the bounds of the law.

Left to fashion a new social order that fit their altered circumstance, women on the frontier made significant changes in their day-to-day living, yet still managed to bring to their new homes a bit of the "civilization" they'd enjoyed in their old ones.

Left: *Across the West, marriage a la façon du pays—according to the custom of the country—was the union of choice for Anglo-Indian couples.*

Below, left: *Only twelve when she married Montana pioneer Granville Stuart, Awbonnie Tookanka, a full-blooded Shoshoni, died at thirty-eight, soon after giving birth to the eleventh child of their twenty-six-year union.*

Below, right: *During his term as U.S. ambassador to Uruguay, Granville Stuart, far left, featured his second wife, Allis Belle, seated at his left.*

Out in Montana Territory, the Ferguses ran into a similar situation. Granville Stuart, one of the region's earliest settlers, was one of many Anglo men who took Indian or mixed-blood women as common-law wives. Unlike Pewter-Eyed Sloan, however, Stuart remained married to Awbonnie Tookanka Stuart for twenty-six years—until she died at age thirty-eight, at which point he mar- ried Allis Belle Brown Fairfield, a one-time teacher at the schoolroom he'd built for the education of his and Awbonnie's eleven children. Shortly after his remarriage, some of his children went to live with his oldest daughter and her husband and some were sent to boarding school at St. Ignatius Mission. Though he continued to provide some financial support for them, personal

Right: *Since romantic alliances between men and women of Hispanic, Native American, African American, and Anglo heritage were generally respected by settlers in the Old Southwest, there was relatively little prejudice toward the children of such alliances—until the arrival of Anglo settlers whose racist and puritanical views of interracial unions cast* barrangia *and marriage* a la façon du pays *in a new and unfavorable light.*

contact with his children was minimal thereafter. Apparently, whatever loyalties he'd felt toward their mother did not extend to them.

According to historian Susan L. Johnson, the cohabitation practiced by Mexican women and Anglo miners living in central Arizona mining towns in the 1860s was viewed by most members of the Mexican working-class culture as "parallel[ing]…formal marriage." Known in medieval Spain as *barrangia*, such unions were particularly popular among people who lacked the money needed to formalize a union and who, lacking wealth or political aspirations, had little reason to be concerned about issues of legitimacy and inheritance.

Apparently the history and significance of *barrangia* meant nothing to the Reverend Hiram Walter Read who, upon finding miner George Clinton sharing quarters with nineteen-year-old Juanita Bachichia, summoned all the residents of Lynx Creek (Arizona) and performed a hasty bilingual wedding ceremony—with George "in his shirt sleeves and Juanita in her morning gown." The scarcity of eligible women in the West meant that courtship between Anglo men and women was often equally swift and to the point. Carpenter William Hiller wrote his wife, Abiah, from California gold country, describing an 1851 wedding that took place "after a long and tedious courtship of some 10 days." During the dance that followed the wedding ceremony, the floor gave way and the guests fell into the hollow beneath the house in a great "pile…made up of the od[d]s and ends of all things in the shape of humanity."

Most Anglos held as much prejudice toward the plural marriages of Mormons as they held toward marriage *à la façon du pays*. Angeline Mitchell Brown recalled an 1870s trip through Arizona Territory in which her family camped "at the Mormon's ranch." Reporting that the man had "2 or else 3 wives," she noted that they saw "16 children sitting on some logs, that seemed to be nearly the same age and size and looked exactly alike" and were "about as wild as quail." Later she saw still more children "22 or 23" in all, though she admitted "I don't suppose they belong to one family."

Behind Closed Doors

Left: *Family portraits such as this one were fairly commonplace among elders in the Church of Jesus Christ of the Latter-day Saints until Congress outlawed polygyny and vowed to withhold statehood until the territory followed suit, at which point Mormon leader Brigham Young— himself the husband of twenty-seven wives and the father of fifty-seven children—issued an edict banning plural marriages.*

Below: *A typical anti-Mormon cartoon of the era depicts a woman's reaction to her husband's having brought home yet another wife*

It is entirely possible that all the children did, indeed, have a single father, since the Latter-day Saints not only sanctioned but actually encouraged plural marriages for those men who had attained a certain level in the church's hierarchy and who could afford to support large families. Brigham Young, the prophet who led the Saints to Zion in the 1840s, is said to have had twenty-seven wives and fifty-seven children himself, having followed the revelation Joseph Smith had received concerning the importance of reestablishing the ancient practice of polygyny. Since a goodly percentage of the early Latter-day Saints had two or more wives, many families found themselves in difficult circumstances when Congress enacted laws against polygamy. Ultimately the church itself issued an 1890 declaration forbidding plural marriages, and after that edict polygyny was no longer officially sanctioned or permitted among its members. *Unofficially,* however, those couples already involved in polygynous unions continued to live as they had always lived—though generally a polygynous husband maintained one home in which he and his first wife lived and one or more homes in which his other wives and children were housed, thereby maintaining the appearance of compliance with the laws of the land and the newly issued edict of the church, while at the same time continuing to fulfill his responsibilities toward *all* of his wives and children.

*Right: For these
Nebraska newlyweds
(above), life in the West
promised the kind of
security, prosperity,
and happiness their
parents and grand-
parents could only have
dreamed of achieving.
When Minnesota pio-
neers Emma Stratton
and David Christie
(below) were married
in Blue Earth County
in the summer of 1870,
they could hardly have
predicted that they
would soon be moving
even farther west—
and that all of their
children would grow up
and be married in
Montana Territory.*

With the exception of Mormon couples, most pioneers married but one spouse at a time in weddings that generally bore at least some resemblance to those back east. Early Mexican-American settlers in the Southwest followed a mixture of Spanish, Mexican, Indian, and Anglo customs in their ceremonies. Mary Barnard Aguirre, who, at eighteen, had married a wealthy Mexican-American trader in a relatively elaborate Anglo-style wedding in the frontier settlement of Kansas City, Missouri, not long thereafter attended a Spanish-American wedding in Las Vegas that she described as "typical of those times in the [Catholic] middle class." After the nuptial ceremony and mass, the wedding party left the church "in a sort of procession with the bride, groom, attendants, and a dozen men, with fiddles and guns. The men played and the guns were fired off at intervals all the way to the grooms house, where a fine breakfast was prepared."

Less than thirty years after the first settlers built homes in Bridger Canyon, the settlement near Bozeman, Montana, where David and Emma Stratton Christie established their homestead, weddings as elaborate as those back in the East were being held by some settlers. When one of the daughters of Abraham and Rachel Grayson Creek was married in 1888, the local newspaper account of the event included a long list of wedding gifts, beginning with a horse and cow provided by the elder Creeks, a parlor stove from a grandparent, and a carpet from the bride's sister. In addition, the pair received six fruit sets, five water sets, two salt castors, two carving sets, two toothpick holders, three silver spoons and holders, and three silver butter dishes—in an era when exchanging duplicate gifts was not likely an acceptable practice.

On a June day some twenty years later, a Bridger Canyon wedding uniting Eva Sparr and Will Christie—one of the five little boys who had ridden the train from Minnesota to Montana with his mother and baby sister in the 1880s—took place in the midst of one of the worst floods ever recorded for the area. A two-day spring storm had dumped twenty-one inches of snow in the canyon, but the sun had popped out and runoff from melting snow filled the creeks to overflowing, taking out all but one bridge in the canyon and turning the roads into gumbo mud that made them nearly impassable. With the bridges out, Will Christie had to swim his team across the creek in order to get into town for the marriage license, and the Bozeman minister who performed the ceremony came as far as he could by carriage, then climbed over a ridge, where he was met by a second carriage that took him to the home of the bride's father, which was festooned with sarvisberry and chokecherry blossoms and filled with excited wedding guests.

Pregnancy and Birth

In the years following, as little Christies began to populate Bridger Canyon, Emma Stratton Christie was on hand for the births of most of her grandchildren, and she served as midwife to many other Bridger Canyon women as well. Bertha Anderson, another Montana homesteader, would have welcomed the help of a neighbor on a day when she suffered a miscarriage while living in a temporary camp where she was cooking for her husband's haying crew. Far from home and with "nothing in the line of clean linen" to use to staunch the bleeding, she grew so weak that she did not move from the tent for three nights and two days, during which time flies "pestered [her] fearfully." On the third day, her husband rode into Sidney and came back with "two women he thought would know about such things." They brought clean linens and "something to stop the flowing, but most of all they brought sympathy." A few days later Bertha was well enough to be taken back home in a "lumber wagon" lined with hay.

Emma Batchelor Lee, a Mormon convert who went to Utah by handcart and became the seventeenth wife of John D. Lee, was alone with her five children when she realized her sixth was about to be born—several weeks earlier than predicted. Instructing her eldest son, Billy, to ask his younger brother to take the three youngest children out "under the tamarack bushes by the corral," well out of earshot of the house, she then explained to Billy that he mustn't be scared if she made a noise since "that always goes with it." After folding a pad and securing it to the bed with safety pins, she got out scissors, string, and a bottle of olive oil; heated a teakettle of water on the stove; and browned flour in the oven. Longing for the company and assistance of "sweet, competent Rachel," one of her husband's senior wives, who had helped her through the birth of her twins, she "prayed she wouldn't die" knowing that "with all those children playing happily outside, she MUST NOT die."

In time, the baby was born, and with the help of her son she tied and cut the umbil-

ical cord, then rubbed the newborn all over with olive oil, sprinkled parched flour on the navel, and pinned on the "belly-band." Billy then carried the placenta outside in the chamber pot and buried it—far from his siblings who were still unaware of the activities in the house. Upon his return, his mother asked him to write his baby sister's birth date—October 25, 1873—"in the Book," then had him invite the younger children in to meet the newest member of the family.

There were times when births were complicated enough that a doctor's services were needed, and when those services were not available, women often died in childbirth. Even an experienced mother like

Above: For most frontierswomen, being so far away from home during pregnancy and childbirth was a particularly trying experience. Often portraits such as this one of Iowa pioneer Esther L. Mendenhall served as baby's first—and sometimes only—introduction to loved ones back east.

Above: The surprise and joy of welcoming these frontier twins was followed by the shock and sorrow of losing them both.

Below: Though blessed with other children, the Harvey Andrews family never ceased to mourn the loss of nineteen-month-old Willie.

Bertha Anderson could not manage on her own when, after two days of labor, her baby refused to be born. The nearest doctor was in Williston, North Dakota, and when he sent word that he could not come for yet another day, the neighbor women who had been assisting settled down to sleep on the floor of the cabin, for "By that time," Anderson recalled, "my pains had eased, and I knew my child was dead." Arriving the next day "dead drunk," the doctor promptly fell down across one of the beds and slept himself sober, at which point he finally "took the child with instruments," a procedure Anderson's neighbor described as "like butchering."

Completing his work, the doctor left Anderson on her own—with the warning that she had "only a slim chance" of surviving. But thanks to the help of her neighbors—and of her husband, who washed her daily with "carbolic water"—infection did not set in and she did, indeed, recover. Her emotional recovery took even longer, and she would "cry and cry for no apparent reason." Though she told the neighbors she was crying for her lost little boy, she remarked in later years that "it was only from weakness," since her precious baby "was well kept" in his heavenly home.

Little Ones Lost

When Oregon pioneer Martha Gay Masterson's little son Freddie died after a sudden and brief illness, the family buried the boy in a place where he loved to play, so that "the little birds he loved in life sang their evening songs over his grave." His little playmates "came loaded with lovely white flowers" which were strewn over his grave. Only a day or so before he grew ill, Masterson had cut his curls for the first time, and asked what should be done with the ringlets, Freddie had answered, "You take one curl, Mama, then I will put the others out by the big tree and the birds can have them to build their nests." Busy with her work, Masterson did not follow him outside and had all but forgotten the incident until late in the fall when one of her daughters called her outside to see a bird's nest she'd found. There in the tangled mass of sticks were little Freddie's golden curls. Twenty-one years later, Masterson still had that little nest.

Native American mothers also experienced the grief of losing a child, though their ceremonies for the dead differed so markedly from those of their Anglo neighbors that cultural clashes were inevitable when the child died in a mission hospital. For example, historian Eleanor Merrow has noted that the Sioux women around Devils Lake Reservation in North Dakota customarily disrobed a child and embraced it moments after its death, then entered into dancing and loud lamentations, followed by a ceremony in which the child's body was suspended horizontally eight or ten feet in the air, a custom that contrasted sharply with the more stately burial customs of the Catholic sisters at the hospital.

Childcare

For mothers of all cultures, keeping little ones healthy and safe in a frontier environment was a major concern. In addition to the general run of childhood illnesses—any of which could be fatal given the wrong turn of events—pioneer women nursed their families through epidemics of cholera, smallpox, diphtheria, and typhoid fever, diseases that came west along with the settlers themselves. For Native American families who had built up no immunity to the common diseases of the Anglos and had no knowledge of how to treat them, measles could be as deadly as smallpox. And, as historian Cornelius J. Jaenen noted, Indians correctly associated the outbreak of such diseases with the influx of Anglos and incorrectly assumed that the transmission of illness was deliberate on the part of the invaders. "It is the Black Robes who make us die by their spells," declared one Canadian Indian

woman, having noted that no one had been sick in their village until the priests came, then "everyone died except for three or four persons." Since the same thing happened when those priests moved on to a second village, she had logically concluded that the Black Robes must be casting evil spells on her people. Indeed, the belief that Anglos generally did all they could to bring illness and death to Indians was so pervasive that when little Sarah Winnemucca became ill after eating too much of a cake that Anglos had given the family, her mother felt sure she'd been poisoned.

Across all cultures, frontier mothers had more than enough to worry about. Since raging rivers, rattlesnakes, farming and mining equipment, hot stoves, steep slopes, and deep forests all provided ample opportunities for accidents that could maim or kill, childcare was an all-consuming task. These special concerns aside, just the day

Below: Though every frontier child had chores to perform, farm life had its rewards.

The Healing Touch

Revered by their own people for their knowledge of spiritual and physical healing, Native American women sometimes shared with settlers their knowledge of herbs and remedies, passed down from their mothers and grandmothers.

Other cultures relied on laywomen as medical practitioners. According to Ann Patton Malone, "no one occupied a higher status [among female slaves] than the Granny-woman." During bondage, these women had made herbal poultices to sooth the wounds of those who had been beaten by their masters. On the frontier, black women used similar poultices to treat wounds from other causes, and they administered herbal remedies and tonics to the sick and debilitated.

Fabiola Cabeza de Baca has noted that although there were no formally trained doctors within two hundred miles of her New Mexico home during her childhood, "every village had its *curandera* or *medica*," a woman well "versed in the curative powers of plants and in midwifery." Plant medicine handed down from the Moors and brought into New Mexico by the earliest Spanish settlers was passed on to each new generation, so that de Baca herself learned the names of "herbs, weeds, and plants that have curative potency."

Anglo pioneer women also used wild plants as medicine. According to May Lacey Crowder, "Culver's root" was taken "for the liver," as were dandelion tea and dandelion wine. Tonics were made from "the butterfly weed, sweet flag root, sassafras bark, and boneset."

to-day necessity of keeping babies and children fed, clothed, warm, dry, entertained, and educated was enough to wear out all but the strongest women, and there were those who found the unrelenting chore less than enjoyable. "It is no pleasure for me to [go] visit[ing] with that crying baby of yours [along]," Lizzie Neblett wrote her husband,

adding, "I think you ought to pay me liberally for raising her." At wits' end, Mary Mahoney confided to her journal, "I am going to get some switches as the boys are crying. They have driven me almost crazy." On the other hand, there were women who took childcare in stride. "I don't see as two babies are any more trouble than one," Kitturah Belknap noted. "I put them both in their little cradle and the little girl amuses the baby till he gets sleepy."

Birth Control—
Limiting One's Blessings

After the birth of her third child, Oregon missionary wife Mary Walker observed, "I find my children occupy much of my time; that if their maker should see fit to withhold from me any more till they require

less of my time and attention, I think I should be reconciled to such an allotment." Unfortunately, Walker had relatively little say over how many children she would ultimately bear, since nineteenth-century birth control methods—short of abstinence— could hardly be depended upon. Large families were considered a blessing and having many children offered some insurance that at least some of them would survive to help with farm and ranching chores and to carry on the family name.

Even so, spacing or limiting one's children was sometimes seen as desirable, at which times women shared certain "secrets" concerning ways of preventing conception. Aside from this woman-to-woman sharing, information was scarce on the frontier, since the Comstock Laws in

Opposite, above: This Silver City, Idaho, child finds comfort in a thumb.

Opposite, below: A blue-ribbon moment at the Custer County Fair.

Below: Having eight children must have been a mixed blessing for any woman not endowed with an endless supply of energy, patience, and shoes!

Below: With their husbands frequently away in the mines or on the open range, frontier wives were often lonely. Many lived miles from their nearest neighbors and had no female friends with whom to discuss the day-to-day dilemmas of marriage and motherhood.

1873 made sending such information through the mails illegal. However, the relative scarcity of extant letters on this most personal of topics probably has far more to do with the unwillingness of women to put such things into writing than with their fear of violating a federal law.

Much of the information on early twentieth-century birth control methods that oral historian Elizabeth Jameson obtained in interviews with women in Colorado mining towns came in oblique statements: "After you went through menopause, you didn't have to worry. You don't have to figure on a calendar and figure up so many days." May Wing, a Boulder resident, noted that women had a wide variety of birth control methods among early settlers: There were those who "used Vaseline a lot," saying "a greased egg wouldn't hatch"; those who practiced the Catholic "rhythm" method, then nursed their babies as long as possible, knowing nursing delayed periods and therefore lessened the chance of conception; and those who used rock salt, something Wing herself never tried, having heard that "it affected the mind." Wing also recalled "a lady that came through [Boulder] one time" and handed a "receipt" for a cocoa butter and boric acid concoction, which was to be mixed well and

molded into "a little cone" to be inserted in the vagina. As birth control became more acceptable, Wing noted that some women answered magazine ads for "a rubber kind of a thing, that you would insert in your vagina. Like a diaphragm."

Malinda Jenkins, a peripatetic westering woman who claimed to have "knowed more about how things was than [most of] the girls around" managed to avoid getting pregnant until an evening when she and her husband went to visit a niece overnight and "didn't carry no paraphernalia because Willie promised to behave hisself." In the end, she reported, "He didn't, and that's where our troubles commenced." The impending pregnancy caused her to have "an awful bad feeling towards Willie," and she later decided that it was no wonder the son she was carrying turned out to be "a tramp and a wanderer" all his life, since, she noted, "He's lived everything I wished for and thought and wanted for myself while I was carrying him."

Though she stated quite frankly that she had but a single thought during that pregnancy—"to run for it, get clear away from everybody"—she appears never to have attempted to abort the baby. Knowledgeable as she claimed to be about such "things," she must have known at least one midwife willing to prepare a potion of herbs and ergot that would have brought on contractions and caused a miscarriage, yet she did not seek such a solution. Though abortion is usually discussed as a phenomenon of the late twentieth century, recipes for "regulating" medications that were to be taken "as long as the occasion demanded" appeared in cookbooks a century ago, as did patent medicines like James Clarke's "Celebrated Female Pills," which were guaranteed to provide "regularity" and clear "Obstructions from any cause whatsoever."

Someone to Talk To

Generally, women in the East learned about such personal things from their neighbors, but women in the West often had no neighbors in whom to confide. Female company had been scarce enough

Far left: Sharing pictures of loved ones back home with an understanding frontier friend.

Left: Keeping in touch with those back east often meant scribbling out a letter in between hanging the wash, weeding the garden, darning socks, and cooking an evening meal.

Below: For most frontier women, finding time to visit with friends sometimes meant combining business with pleasure— with one woman reading aloud while the others kept their fingers busy with knitting, mending, or crocheting.

for Annie Green when she lived in Greeley, Colorado, but her troubles "commenced in earnest" when she moved eight miles out of town to live on the ranch land her husband had laid claim to. "This had truly been the longest and most dreary week of my life," she wrote from their shanty, "and the first one without seeing and talking with those of my own sex." Louisa Cook of Boise, Idaho, complained in the fall of 1863 that she had "but two or three Lady acquaintances in this country," for although there were "a great many in all the mining towns who [wore] the form of woman," most were "o so fallen and vile, a living, burning shame to the sex they have so disgraced" and true "*Ladies* [were] not plenty." While Cook refused the company of Boise women of low society, Mary Hallock Foote complained about the women of high society in that same town, saying they "had ridiculous social pretensions and showed bad taste in their attempts to imitate what they conceived to be the latest Eastern fashions."

When Pamelia Fergus moved to the isolated central Montana ranch that was to be her final home, her nearest neighbor was Granville Stuart's Indian wife. Since Awbonnie Tookanka Stuart spoke but little English and Pamelia Fergus knew her neighbor's language not at all, communi-

cation between the two would have been limited, and it is doubtful they ever conversed on matters of feminine health and hygiene, though scholars have discovered that Native American women often expressed curiosity about such things. Maria Chona, a Papago woman, was puzzled because she'd never seen white women segregate themselves each month and wondered if they, too, went through "that thing...which happens to all our women....It is called menses."

Above: For the Neelys of Lane County, Oregon, music lent comfort, warmth, and cheer to cold and dreary winter evenings. Here, the sounds of popping corn and crackling fire were descant to the melody of the violin and organ duet performed by father and daughter.

Anglo women did, indeed, experience "that thing" of which Maria Chona spoke, and, as historian Glenda Riley noted, many a patent medicine peddler made money by selling various and sundry pharmaceuticals to combat menstrual cramps and other "female weaknesseses." Yellow Dock Sasparilla was touted as a cure-all for "female troubles" in general, while Dr. Duponco's Golden Periodical Pills for Females were supposed to ease menstrual pain. Husbands and children were also frequently dosed with patent medicines, which were advertised widely in almanacs and in the women's magazines of the day.

Frontier Entertainment
The magazines that carried those advertisements were an important link to the world back east. Henrietta Embree reported that she'd "read Godeys Ladies book nearly thru," paying special attention to the latest eastern fashions depicted on its pages. Carrie Williams was more inter-

ested in the stories on that magazine's pages, finding comfort in tales such as "Margaret's Home," an account of "the trials of Margaret the good and patient," a hardworking, long-suffering woman whose life eventually came to a "happy conclusion."

The Bible was read in many western homes, and for some women, church socials and other religious functions were a focal point. For Mary Barnard Aguirre, the christening of her son, Pedro, at La Mesilla was a high point of her early years in New Mexico. Afterwards, there was a grand supper, during which "Pedro was set at the head of the table and crowed and laughed in a wonderful way for a six months old baby." Then his father held him aloft and "his health was drunk by all." The dance that followed this supper went on into "the 'wee wee hours' and every one enjoyed and long remembered Pedros christening."

Outdoor events were also fun for families, with sleighing, skiing, and skating being wintertime favorites, while picnics, swimming, fishing, and camping were enjoyed in warmer months. Bessie Stratton Turner, one of Emma Christie's neighbors in Bridger Canyon, recalls setting out for Yellowstone National Park in late June of 1913, a trip of around one hundred miles that can be made by car today in a couple of hours but took Turner's group nearly a week, since they had to stop frequently to cut and move trees that had fallen across the road or to dig their way out of deep mudholes. Once they entered the park, they were temporarily stranded when some of their horses started back toward Bozeman, but the animals were quickly rounded up and the group moved on to Old Faithful, then wound its way out of the park by way of Livingston, where they met a neighbor who told them a dance would be held that evening at a home in the canyon.

Hurrying the last thirty miles, they made it home in time to attend the dance and share with their neighbors the details of their adventure in Yellowstone.

While Turner does not name the couple who hosted that particular dance, the Bridger Canyon home of John and Frances Wittman was the scene of many Saturday night gatherings in which twenty to thirty people would convene for an evening of square dancing to fiddle, piano, and guitar accompaniment. Wittman recalled preparing "a washtub of sandwiches" for one such party, and she remembered another gathering on a night when the temperature dropped to thirty below zero, but the dancing continued until dawn while the children slept on stacks of coats in a back bedroom. With the coming of the first light, everyone bundled up and started for home—in time to attend to the morning chores.

Below: Seated on a boardwalk shared by a lounging cat, a woman awaits her turn at croquet. As their elegant hats, ruffled blouses, and brocaded skirts attest, these Iowa frontierswomen were every bit as fashion-conscious as their eastern sisters.

Below: Bundled well against Nebraska's numbing winter winds and wearing the strap-on skates of the era, these Cherry County pioneers enjoy an afternoon on the ice.

Mary Hopping, an Idaho pioneer, recalled a festive evening on which a woman holding a baby was asked to dance and promptly "plumped her baby down in [the] lap [of a] batchelor…sitting nearby," saying "'Hold this youngin' while I dance and if he cries you wallop 'im.'" When no musicians were available or in those settlements where dancing was frowned upon by certain religious groups, "play parties" featuring such singing games as Skip-to-My-Lou, Pig in the Parlor, and Bounce Around were popular. Late in the evening, the more daring might engage in a round of Weevily Wheat, a "game" considered too much like "real dancing" to be deemed appropriate by more conservative church members.

Dancing and singing were favorite pastimes of Mormon emigrants—from Salt Lake City to the smallest town settled by these zealous converts. Brigham Young himself encouraged the development of theatrical talents in the young people of the church and authorized the construction of a theater, where he and his wives and daughters could often be observed looking down on pageants or plays from a series of boxes perpetually reserved for their use.

As historian Sandra Myres observed, women on the Hispanic frontier enjoyed parties, fiestas, and *bailes* or dances featuring the breaking of *cascarones*, egg shells filled with silver and gold confetti and sweet-smelling liquids. They also enjoyed traditional secular and religious plays such as *Los Pastores*, which one California settler described as "a religious comedy" featuring such characters as "an Angel, the Devil, a Hermit, a Bartelo." *Jacalear*, or the custom of paying calls on one's neighbors, was another way westering women in the Southwest passed the time.

Holiday Celebrations

Though glad to have good neighbors with whom to celebrate, pioneer women missed their friends and relatives back east, especially during holiday celebrations. Christmas celebrations out west usually mimicked those enjoyed back home in Iowa or Missouri or New England. This was difficult in areas where there were no evergreen trees to be found, but Sadie Martin was so determined to have a tree for little Brayton that she brought in a branch from a mesquite tree, reporting that "when it was decorated with silver balls made of cotton, covered with tinfoil (which came with tobacco or cigars) and strings of popcorn, and other home made decora-

Behind Closed Doors

Left: In a dual celebration of warm spring weather and the Easter holiday, several residents of Riverside, New Mexico, enjoy an outdoor egg boil. The woman in charge of the outing may well have been explaining the colors yielded by various vegetable dyes—onion skins for reddish brown, carrot peels for bright orange, carrot tops for spring green. With only a scatter of leaves to impede her course, the woman in the photo's center has found this lovely site wheelchair accessible.

tions, it all looked very lovely to us." A few years later, Sadie and her husband John decided to throw a community-wide Christmas party at which sixty-five people dined on "an immense piece of beef and a whole pig" cooked in a pit her husband dug in their yard. The neighbors brought cakes, pies, and bread, and one of them dressed as Santa and presented "little trinkets to each child in attendance."

Mary Barnard Aguirre and her husband—who was "much beloved in the town"—were once invited to serve as "Padrinos," or godparents, for New Year's Eve high mass. Seated on chairs in front of the altar, they held "highly decorated wax candles," and Aguirre noted, "These were lit and my whole attention was devoted to keeping that candle straight—for I was so interested with the newness of every thing that I'd forget the candle for a moment and it would bob over to the imminent danger of my hat."

Family Friction

Wallace Williams not only played the fiddle but also played the cornet, and he and his father were both members of the Union Brass Band, which often opened shows at the local theater. Both men also belonged to a local lodge, and while the men were out practicing, performing, or attending lodge meetings, Carrie and her mother-in-law were at home, keeping house and tending to little Wally. "O how I wish he would give up going to town so much evenings on one pretext or another and stay with me and I would lay my head in his lap and read to him as I used to do," Carrie confided to her diary. Noting that her husband's "whole time and attention" were given to "practic[ing] music to play with the band," she observed that they hardly spoke more than a dozen words to each other in a day and lamented that the two of them had "no pursuits in common…anymore."

On an evening when he "finally decided to stay home…he went and got his horn and rendered [the] night hideous about here with the thing." When he responded to her complaints by going outside, she noted that he was "down to the chicken pen…with that odious horn" and ultimately concluded, "I think he is wasting his life fast away blowing that everlasting cornet." Predictably, the couple soon began to quarrel, and after he left home one morning before she could put breakfast on the table she admitted, "Him and I had some trouble this morning; therefore his hurry to get away, though he said he had an engagement to play."

While it was Carrie Williams who nagged her husband for his annoying habits, it was Elkanah Walker who nagged his wife Mary about the many things he found problematic in her behavior—so many, in fact, that on one occasion Mary signed a letter "your loving but not always obedient wife" and once noted that she was "almost in despair and without hope of his ever being pleased or satisfied with [her]" and feared that she could "never, with all [her] care, make [her]self what he would like [her] to be."

Above: *As their friend relaxes on the rocks above, two anglers attempt to entice a trout by dangling worms from lines attached to makeshift fishing poles.*

Carrie Williams recalled a Nevada Territory New Year's Eve candy-pulling party in which several girls sang to the accompaniment of a flute, then Carrie's husband, Wallace, got out his fiddle and those present danced "the old fashioned french four," kicking up "a terrible dust." Little Wally, her son, "act[ed] so cunningly" that she "[could] not refrain from speaking about it." As the musicians played, the little boy "kept his body going to and fro, till he would get tired. Then he would keep his hands going up and down, keeping perfect time with the music." Reporting that "it was quite amusing to see him perform," she noted that he did not go to sleep until "1/2 after ten" and she herself didn't turn in until one o'clock, at which time she sat down to write an account of the evening, ending with, "So passed off New Year's day 1859 in this house, district of Gold Flat, County of Nevada."

Indeed, after her husband's death she penned the following penitent lines in her journal:

> And now I recollect with pain
> The many times I grieved him sore,
> Oh if he would but come again
> I think I'd vex him so no more.

Not "vexing" a man like Elkanah would have posed problems, judging from his expectations of a wife, as set forth in a letter he wrote to her:

> I want someone to get me a good supper and let me take my ease and when I am very tired in the morning I want someone to get up and get breakfast and let me lay in bed and take my rest. More than all I want my wife where I can have her company and to cheer me up when the blue devils chain me down.

Equally blunt concerning his expectations of his wife, Pamelia, James Fergus made it clear that he would tolerate no insubordination, especially in front of friends. A few days after a dinner party at which Pamelia had stood up to him when he complained that she'd oversalted the food, James wrote her a lengthy letter, declaring that "a good woman" would have responded by saying that she "felt sorry that such was the case, would say that she would try to be more careful in the future and would try [to do] so," while Pamelia had dared to "stir up discord" by saying "it was *not* too salt[y]." Since the woman to whom he was writing had spent the last four years managing all the family's affairs on her own back in Little Falls, it is doubtful that James's last-ditch effort to restore the old order of command had much effect on Pamelia's behavior in subsequent years—though she may have been more careful about contradicting her husband in public.

Upon hearing that his daughter Mary Agnes and her husband, Robert Hamilton, were experiencing marital difficulties, James apparently assumed that Mary Agnes had followed her mother's example. "Don't talk back so much to Robert," he warned

her. "When he abuses you with his tongue, let him go on." He did not, however, advise her to endure physical abuse and warned his son-in-law, "I never expected you to agree well because you could not agree when single, but I did not expect it to come to throwing sticks of wood to telling her to go home, etc., etc."

Separation and Divorce

While there were many wives who endured even physical abuse in silence, feeling they would never be able to support themselves and their children without a husband and knowing that divorced women were generally looked down upon by society, there were others who rose up against abusive husbands and ultimately managed to escape a bad marriage. Western states were the most liberal in establishing grounds for divorce, with Indiana and South Dakota

Below: Born in Helena, Montana Territory, in 1869, Grace Fisk was "fearless and independent" at twelve, "womanly and self-reliant" at sixteen, married at twenty-one, and divorced at thirty. In this 1899 photo she lifts her glass high— perhaps in celebration of her recently regained freedom, perhaps in defiance of the teachings of her WCTU mother.

Mining Widows on the Frontier

With spring avalanches a yearly worry, cave-ins a constant threat, and explosions a frequent occurrence, many a miner's wife sent her husband off to work wondering whether or not she would ever see him alive again. Concerned as they were over the situation, the women could do little more than fret, since there was virtually no regulation of safety for mining on the early frontier. Indeed, accidents of any sort were more often than not attributed to the carelessness of their victims.

Coal mines were particularly dangerous, since the powdery dust could explode at the slightest spark. When an 1884 explosion of unknown origin sent flames racing through the lower levels of the Colorado Coal and Iron Company's Crested Butte mine, families and friends rushed to the scene, hoping against hope to find their loved ones alive and well. Those not so fortunate then began the interminably long wait associated with such events, as the fire had to burn itself out before the mine could be ventilated so that the dead and injured could be retrieved without the loss of still more lives. One by one the bodies of the men were brought forth from the mine and laid out in a shed to be identified by friends and family. In all, sixty workers were either burned to death or suffocated.

Though owners rarely admitted liability for the deaths of their workers, one of the copper kings of Butte, Montana, did establish an orphanage for children whose fathers were lost or severely injured in his mine, and by the latter part of the nineteenth century, increased pressure from such groups as the United Mine Workers resulted in token payments to the families of victims.

passing lenient divorce laws even before Reno, Nevada, became the city of choice for divorcing spouses.

Though separation and divorce were increasingly common in the nineteenth century, many women avoided divorce because of the social stigma it still carried, others because it was against their religious beliefs, and still others because divorcing threatened their economic security. Catholic Mexican-American marriages in the Southwest were often annulled, restoring single status to each of the parties involved without going against the church's edict against divorce. According to historian Maryann Oshanna, within Native American cultures, a woman's status following separation from her husband depended upon her tribal customs. In matrilineal tribes women remained in the home and retained control and custody of the children, since women had the right to control all "property."

Unfortunately, since most western women lived in patriarchal systems in which husbands had control of all property, divorce often left women in dire straits.

Kate Carmack, one of the wealthiest of the Klondike women, had been a partner in her husband George's mining interests from the first, yet when she sued him for divorce and demanded her half of their $1.5 million estate, George managed to keep all the money by claiming he and Kate had never been legally married. She returned to her home in the Yukon and lived out her days on a government pension.

With their economic status so threatened by divorce, many women remained married "for the sake of the children"—even when the children were being abused. However, there were times when a husband's abuse of a child pushed an otherwise timid woman into action. Oregon emigrant Elizabeth Paschal Dillon Gay's first husband was "a skillful surgeon and a good doctor when he was sober" but when he was drunk, "which was most of the time," he would worry their little girl "until she cried and then he would beat her for crying." With life "so impossible," Elizabeth took Jesse and fled to another town, but when Dillon followed her and promised "never [to] touch another drop," she "took him back." Several more years passed before she decided it was "hopeless to try to live with [her] husband" any longer, and in April of 1865 she finally sought and secured a divorce.

Though Elizabeth Gay took her daughter with her when she left her husband, Malinda Jenkins left her little ones behind, though she had never before "been away from them a day." Having "stud[ied] it out" during a severe illness from which she nearly died, she'd realized that "staying there meant hardship and want for the rest of [her] life." Deciding she wanted "a chance to find something else for [her] children," she'd promised God she'd do just that if she could just get well.

Since secrecy was essential, she told the children nothing about her plan but simply "washed their little feet and cleaned them up like always, before I put them to bed and kissed them good night," telling them only that she was going to see their aunt down in Texas and would be back to "fetch them." After several years of working hard all day and crying herself to sleep each night, Jenkins took a friend's advice and married a wealthy older man who promised to support her in a legal fight to regain her children.

Sometimes women separated from their husbands without benefit of formal divorce proceedings. At the end of twenty years of marriage, Martha Gay Masterson declared that she had made her last move and told her peripatetic husband to go on without her, which he apparently did. Her memoir makes no mention of a formal divorce. Similarly, after seventeen years of wandering from one western town to another, Rena Matthews's mother "obtained a separation and settled in Sacramento."

Bonded by Adversity

Though divorce was more frequent in the West than in the East during the nineteenth and early twentieth century, many pioneering couples found that laboring long and hard together under less than ideal circumstances tended to cement, rather than

erode, a relationship. Despite the disquiet James and Pamelia Fergus experienced after he accused her of oversalting the food and she swore at him in exasperation, the later years of their marriage were, according to James, their happiest years. "We were always together," he wrote to one of their daughters shortly after Pamelia's death, "and thought far more of each other than we did when we were young. I think people of good sense generally do, haveing lived so long together they become so used to each others ways become more like each other are more forgiving and one becomes as it were a necessity to the other. I know it was so for us."

Since we have no written record to indicate that his wife would have disagreed with his evaluation of the dynamics of their lengthy relationship, we can conclude that at least for this particular couple, the shared burdens of establishing a new home in the West fostered unity by developing a sense of mutual pride in what a husband and wife had accomplished during their years of sacrifice and hard work. Thus, though James Fergus had once taken his wife's labors so much for granted that he'd offered advice as to what she should do "now that she had leisure," in their final years together he praised her for having "done her full share towards raising our family, procuring a living and acquiring what property we possess," thereby at least acknowledging the value and importance of the work of woman's hands.

Above, left and right: Though Montana pioneers Pamelia and James Fergus experienced their share of marital friction during their years of struggle on the frontier, in the end they seemed to have been bonded by adversity, so that James, who had once taken Pamelia's hard work for granted, came at last to praise her for having "done her full share" in establishing a homestead in the county that bears the Fergus name.

The Work of Women's Hands

Pioneer Women in Action

In her well-known memoir, *A Bride Goes West*, Nannie Alderson noted that life grew increasingly difficult once she reached her new home in Montana Territory, "[for] I was no longer a bride who went west, nor a woman who was helping to open up a new country: I was merely an overworked mother of four, trying to make ends meet under conditions which were none too easy."

Her hard work notwithstanding, Alderson would have been one of the thousands of wives and mothers who census takers listed as "not gainfully employed." As historian Glenda Riley noted, even though frontierswomen did all the cooking, cleaning, and childcare essential to a household's survival and often engaged in the manufacture of soap, cloth, candles, and clothes (items that were being produced in factories and purchased in stores by women back east) their domestic skills were undervalued because the services performed and goods produced were for the benefit of the family rather than for wages or for sale in the marketplace.

Rosalyn Baxandall, Linda Gordon, and Susan Reverby point out in *America's Working Women* that the work a woman did to care for her children and spouse and keep the household running was generally "seen as part of the natural functions of the universe, as instinctive as an animal building a nest, as little noticed as breathing." Yet without that work, none of the *men's* work usually associated with frontier living could have been accomplished, and a study of the work done by working-class pioneer women leaves little doubt that they were gainfully employed at work of significant economic value to the households in which they labored.

Furthermore, as historian Julie Roy Jeffrey has observed, for most pioneers, "The first years of settlement…continued the trail experience by demanding that women depart from cultural and social behavioral norms for the sake of their family's survival." Thus the work of a pioneer woman included not only the work she'd traditionally done in the East but also whatever additional work was required in order to ensure the success of new enterprises in the West—including such traditionally

Opposite: *With wood running low inside the house, Norah Clough saws a log into stove-wood lengths.*

Below: *For this Texas emigrant, carding and spinning wool were ongoing tasks.*

Above: *With no oxen at hand, these Russian immigrants form their own team to till the soils of Saskatchewan.*

Opposite, above: *A monument to the back-breaking job of gleaning the rocks and stones turned up by plow and spade.*

Opposite, below: *In this turn-of-the-century photo made with film too slow to compensate for the movement caused by the unceasing winds of the Iowa plains, Addie Marsh's laundry seems to all but disappear.*

"male" chores as digging cellars and plowing fields. Indeed, frontier women "not only had quilting bees but [had] bees to build houses, dig canals, and erect fences."

It is important to realize that few nineteenth-century women would have viewed this situation as "liberating," since engaging in more work—even "men's work"—generally meant having less free time in which to pursue whatever leisure activities a woman of that era might have enjoyed pursuing, from reading the latest issue of *Godey's Lady's Book* to writing letters to far-distant friends and relatives. Even so, in some cases women who were obliged to cross gender lines and perform chores that would customarily have been reserved for males found this experience empowering. This proved to be the case for Pamelia Fergus, whose husband James had predicted, "My going away has [been] and will be of great benefit to you, by throwing you on your own resources and learning you to do business for yourself."

Though Pamelia hardly saw her husband's abrupt departure for the goldfields in the spring of 1860 as anything to be grateful for, ultimately his assertion that

she would attain new growth by being left to manage on her own during his absence proved to be fairly accurate. For example, when it came time to pay taxes, Pamelia tried at first to leave that task to a male family friend, writing James, "I know nothing about these things onley they have to be payed if they are advertised…I go [about town] but little [and] h[ear] but little of mans bussiness but I saw something in the paper that called my attention to it." Though she declared, "I did not know what to do," ultimately she braved the stares of the men of Little Falls and dared to go into the courthouse herself to find out what was owed. While she still did not have the money she needed to pay the taxes, she'd taken the first step toward doing so, and upon her return she wrote James, "I only had to regret I had not went before."

While Pamelia Fergus and thousands of other wives whose husbands left them behind in order to seek their fortunes in the West learned valuable coping skills during their stints as women in waiting on the home frontier, thousands of other women learned similar survival skills during the long journey westward. The remainder—

those who traveled west by water or rail and missed the lessons of the overland trail—received "on the job" training once they arrived on the frontier.

Training, however it was obtained, proved useful, for pioneer women not only attended to their accustomed domestic chores, plus whatever outdoor labors were required but—far removed as they were from the constraints of eastern propriety—they also occasionally ventured out into the world of commerce, sometimes undertaking work they would never have dreamed of attempting under any other circumstances.

Women's Work—Frontier Style

"Women's work," frontier style, like women's work on the trail, included all of the household chores of women back east without the conveniences those women had begun to enjoy. Thus it is little wonder that Oregon pioneer Abigail Scott Duniway quickly concluded, "To bear two children in two and a half years…to make thousands of pounds of butter every year for market, not including what was used…at home, to sew and cook, and wash

Above: Having spent the morning cooking a hearty noon meal, this Arizona mother and daughter attend to dishwashing chores, using water heated in a kettle on the stove.

Below: For this New Mexican woman, baking meals in a hornilla *was a well-practiced art.*

and iron; to bake and clean and stew and fry; to be, in short, a general pioneer drudge, with never a penny of my own, was not pleasant business."

Bertha Anderson, who traveled from Denmark to Montana by ship and rail in the 1880s, found that even the traditional work of women's hands—cooking, housekeeping, washing, and childcare—was far more difficult in her new circumstances. Meal preparation posed the first challenge; she had only "tin dishes from the ship" when she arrived, though soon thereafter a neighbor loaned her a kettle and frying pan. Like most frontier women, Anderson made do with whatever was on hand—

rolling out pie crusts with glass bottles, churning milk in gallon cans, and cooking over open fires or in fireplaces, adjusting recipes for the uneven heat.

Anderson, like other women on the frontier, found particularly frustrating the fact that the men in the family were often too busy doing outside chores to give their attention to improving working conditions indoors. According to Harriet Taylor Upton, author of a 1910 history of the Ohio Reserve, one woman finally grew so tired of baking all her bread and doing all her cooking in "one big iron kettle" that she gave up on her procrastinating husband, "fashioned some bricks of mud," and built herself an oven "which was such a success that people travelled out of their way to see it in action."

Historian Sylvia Van Kirk has noted that Native American women, like most Anglo pioneer women, were in charge of gathering, processing, preparing, and preserving food for themselves and their families. Women in northwestern tribes skinned the animals killed in the hunt, cut the meat into thin strips, and dried it over a slow fire or in the sun before pounding it into a thick, flaky mass and mixing it with melted buffalo fat and dried berries to make pemmican. They then packed the pemmican into buffalo-hide sacks they'd made during the winter for this purpose.

Mexican women who were accustomed to cooking over outdoor fires shared their knowledge with Anglo brides who moved into their communities, showing the newcomers how to cook in a *hornilla*. But such assistance wasn't always enough to stave off feelings of panic and inadequacy. When faced with the challenge of cooking over an open fire, Guadalupe Callan's mother burst into tears, then retreated to the house, where she "picked up an ostrich fan, a relic of past grandeur, and fanned herself," leaving her daughters to cope with the task at hand.

Rachael Whitfield, a Texan freed from slavery by the Emancipation Proclamation, made do with "an old cracked pitcher, a flat wooden pail with a metal rim and lid, a basket…and a big, long and deep iron baking

or roasting vessel with a lid." Using these implements, Whitfield and her daughters "made hominy, 'chitlings,' and ash cakes; roasted eggs, sweet potatoes, and cushaw; boiled cabbage, beans, turnips, collards, okra, and hamhocks, and made corn bread and biscuit." Taking what they could from the land, they picked wild plums and berries for preserves; trapped birds, squirrels, and possums; and gathered prairie chicken eggs.

Housekeeping on the frontier proved to be as challenging as cooking. Kaia Cosgriff, who traveled from Norway to Montana as a child, recalled for oral historian Donna Gray the difficulties her mother had in carrying out her day-to-day cleaning chores when she only "had two apple boxes in the corner" to serve as a cupboard and had no broom or mop for cleaning the floor. "When my mother would want to sweep the floor," Cosgriff noted, "she'd take an ax and go out and chop the sagebrush…[for the broom] she'd sweep the floor with."

Though housekeeping has generally been taken for granted or seen as something women *enjoyed* doing, some pioneers were frank about how they felt about the business of keeping a house clean and neat. Madge Walker of Pray, Montana, recalled how much she disliked washing the separator, a daily chore for women involved in making butter and cheese. "I hated it," she recalled, though she admitted, "I think it was more because everybody said, 'Oh, the separator is so bad!' There was so much talk [that] I thought I should dislike it, too." Whether or not she liked cleaning the separator, it was one of several tasks "you *had* to do…like cleaning up the lamps in the morning.…You had to put the kerosene in and trim the wicks and wash the chimney.… that's one of the first things you did if you were a good housekeeper."

Laundry was another thing one "*had* to do." Many pioneer women made their own soap, a laborious and odoriferous process that involved pouring water through fireplace ashes to make lye, which was then mixed with leftover household grease, brought to a boil, and stirred constantly

until the moment when the soap "came" and could be dipped into a barrel or can. Doing laundry required water as well as soap, and those women who had no wells either hauled water from springs or streams or used what they'd caught in rain barrels whose scanty supply must serve the family for other purposes as well.

Sometimes it was easier to take the clothes to a nearby stream, and historian Sandra Myres noted that one Mexican-American woman recalled childhood memories of washdays in which she and her siblings, plus all the family's clothes and bedding, were piled into a large *carreta* and driven to a hot springs some distance away where "columns of white steam rose among the oaks, and the precious waters, which were strong with sulphur, were seen flowing over the crusted basin." While children found such excursions fun, their mothers usually did not. One pioneer reported feeling "worse than a stewed witch" after a day spent over a laundry tub.

The clothes women washed and ironed were often clothes they had made or mended themselves, since moving to the frontier meant moving away from ready access to dressmakers, tailors, and milliners, and few pioneers could afford to order their clothes from back east or to buy them from the relatively few stores that served most frontier settlements. Even

Above: *Following a recipe handed down through several generations, this Oregon pioneer engages in the time-honored spring ritual of making soap. Lye made by leaching water through ashes is added to grease, mixed well, and boiled. As the soap "comes," it is skimmed off and poured into a tin bucket, then into wooden boxes lined with cloth. The hardened soap is cut into bars and stored. Laundry soap was usually dark and unscented, but some women made a whiter hand and dish soap by using pure beef tallow and scenting the soap with rose petals or lavender.*

97

Right: The work of manufacturing the family's clothes went faster when neighbors helped each other card the wool or comb the flax that was to be spun into thread. Flax was then woven into linen cloth, wool into woolen cloth, or both into linsey-woolsey, all of which could be colored with indigo or vegetable dyes before being hand- or machine-stitched into pants, shirts, and dresses.

Below: Long skirts flying, two eastern Oregon women circle back to round up a few stragglers in a cattle drive across the open range.

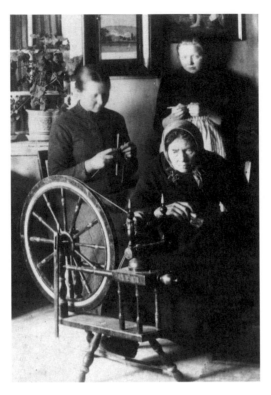

well into the twentieth century, homesteading women were making and mending the family's clothes, though as Helen Seright recalled, "I didn't have very much time to do any fancy work when [the children] were growing up."

Many women carded and spun wool from the sheep they'd helped to raise, then knit warm socks and sweaters for themselves and their families. Warm as they were, wool stockings were not always comfortable, particularly for children with allergies, though

such ailments were so little understood in those days that when young Kaia Cosgriff complained that her stockings made her itch, her mother dismissed her complaint, declaring, "Kaia's the fussiest thing! She always fusses about everything."

Making clothing for the family was a chore for Native American women as well, and Buffalo Bird Woman, a Hidatsa who grew up along the banks of the Missouri in present-day North Dakota, recalled learning how "to dress skins, embroider, sew with awl and sinew" and to cut and make moccasins, clothing, and tent covers.

Homesteading Heroics

Pamelia Fergus had always been in primary charge of the family's garden and orchard in Little Falls, Minnesota, and after James set out for Pikes Peak she took on the supervision of all other farming and livestock operations as well. For a while after her arrival in Montana Territory, she relinquished most of the heavy outside work she had undertaken out of necessity, but when James entered politics and began spending long weeks away from home, she began handling all the business associated with running the stage station the couple operated on the Mullan Road near Helena.

Other women who had crossed gender lines to take on "men's work" in the absence of their westering husbands or on the way west were often obliged to continue that

The Work of Women's Hands

work once they reached their new homes on the frontier, since whenever there was no man around when it came time for a job to be done, women were obliged to do it. This could include anything from plowing fields to digging storm cellars and wells, from slaughtering and dressing chickens to milking cows.

Though pioneer women in western Oregon were undertaking such chores by the early 1840s, many of the women on the last homesteading frontier—western North and South Dakota, the central and eastern portions of Oregon, Washington, and Montana—were still pioneering well into the twentieth century. According to oral historian Laurie K. Mercier, improved dryland farming methods, the Enlarged Homestead Act of 1909, and the promotional activities of states, railroads, and developers lured tens of thousands of people west in search of land suitable for farming and ranching. Handwritten transcripts of interviews with many of these latter-day pioneers were made by Works Progress Administration employees during the 1930s. Over the past few decades, oral historians have been capturing the voices of these setters in taped interviews that have been invaluable to scholars seeking a better understanding of the work of women in farming and ranching.

As Mercier has noted, the oral reminiscences of these women reveal details of

their work in the day-to-day operations of farms and ranches. Like pioneers a century earlier, these women were often obliged to take on such chores as threshing, branding, and haying, and Katie Adams remarked, "I was just like a hired man. I was right there. I helped harness the horses and unharness them and hitch them up, and I followed the plow more than once, and the harrow and the rake, raked the fields. I done a lot of it." Homesteader Dorothy Johnston noted that she "could

Left: Arizona settler Sharlot Hall plays mother to a quintet of hungry piglets.

Below: Colorado ranch women grain the mare and throw cracked corn to a mixed flock of turkeys and chickens.

Gardens Are for Singing:

Waheenee, a Hidatsa woman, recalled that in her tribe, "the labor of clearing the ground for cornfields was done chiefly by the women, although the older men helped." Soon after camp was pitched, Waheenee's grandmother would choose a site and lead the women in clearing a field. When the ground was ready, the women would plant seed corn, squash, beans, and sunflowers. Crows were a major problem, and Waheenee and the other children were often sent out to chase the birds away. At one point, her grandmother made a scarecrow by driving two sticks into the ground for legs and binding "two sticks to them for arms." Then she fastened on "a ball of castaway skins for a head" and belted on an old robe. "Such a scarecrow looked wicked!" Waheenee recalled, "Indeed I was almost afraid of it myself."

The crows, however, were not, and soon the young women in the tribe were sent to the field to build platforms or stages made of split logs supported by four beams about as high as full-grown stalks of corn. From the "watchers' stage" in her mother's field, Waheenee and her sister, Cold Medicine, kept an eye out for hungry crows, horses that might break into the field and trample the stalks, or boys who "might steal the green ears and go off and roast them." While they watched they sang, for their people thought "that the corn plants had souls, as children have souls, and that the growing corn liked to hear us sing, as children like to hear their mothers sing to them."

run all of the farm machines; I could run the mowers and the combines and the rakes and I knew how to irrigate…[and] all that stuff that goes with it."

Many homestead women milked cows, and many women in the West still milk cows, though few milk more than one or two cows by hand anymore. Montana ranchwoman Ethel Briggs began milking at age nine or ten, and for most of her married life she milked a number of cows, taking a five-gallon can of cream into town to sell every week and using the money it brought to buy groceries and gas. In later years, she noted, "These days, three cows is all I'm milking, because my tendonitis kinda gets to flaring up if I milk any more." Even so, she intended to "keep milking as long as I'm able, because in the wintertime I'm afraid I'd get so lazy, I'd be in a wheelchair if I didn't have that!" Admitting that when it was "awfully cold" it was "miserable to go out and milk a cow," she recalled mornings so cold "you have to put your hands up between the bag and their flank to kinda get the frost off the top of your hand." But the inveterate dairy woman declared, "All in all, I don't mind milking."

The Work of Women's Hands

Many farm women had total charge of the raising of chickens or turkeys. "My mother had a few chickens and I knew there was money in chickens," recalled homesteader Anna Lehfeldt. "It was a way of income, we could trade the eggs for food and provisions and different things." Other women cared for gardens and orchards. When the dam and irrigation system that kept the family's orchard watered were lost in a flood, Mormon emigrant Emma Lee threw herself into the arduous task of lugging buckets of water in order to save the trees from drought.

Single women who homesteaded by themselves did all the farming chores—plus anything else that had to be done to keep their claims in good standing. According to a study done by Paula M. Nelson, between 1900 and 1915 only 8 out of 220 homesteading women on the South Dakota frontier were engaged in farming full-time. Most of the remaining 212 women also worked as teachers or domestics, driving out to their holdings only often enough to keep the Land Office pacified.

Erikka Hansen, a young teacher who moved from her parents' home in eastern South Dakota to claim a homestead in the southwestern corner of that state, lived in a tar-paper shack with shingled roof and worked a small garden with her only tool—

a hoe. Since her farming income was minimal, she taught in area schools, boarding out with families during the school term and only spending summers and occasional weekends on her claim.

Determined to make a home for herself and her daughter, Colorado homesteader Elinore Pruitt Stewart, a widow, handled all the household chores, herded cattle, plowed fields, planted and harvested crops, and ultimately came to conclude:

> To me, homesteading is the solution of all poverty's problems, but I realize that temperament has much to do with success in any undertaking, and persons afraid of coyotes and work and loneliness had better let ranching alone. At the same time, any woman who can stand her own company, can see the beauty of the sunset, loves growing things, and is willing to put in as much time at careful labor as she does over the washtub, will certainly succeed; will have independence, plenty to eat all the time, and a home of her own in the end.

Many a homesteader who had once shared Stewart's optimism was ultimately defeated by problems beyond her control. During the drought of 1911, with no grass

Above: *Having hobbled her cow, a Montana ranch woman splashes bag and teats with water before beginning to milk. Milking in the pasture was a summertime-only option in a state with winter wind chills of forty below.*

Opposite: *Turn-of-the-century Iowans proudly display shocks of freshly harvested grain.*

Right: Clara Brown, a freed slave from Kentucky, used the $10,000 she earned doing gold-rush laundry to help other ex-slaves find work in Colorado.

Below: A streamlined Iowa laundry operation—complete with store-bought soap, a vat and stick for boiling white clothes, and a washtub with scrub board and wringer.

Opposite, above: In the West, as in the East, a servant "girl's" duties, treatment, and wages depended upon the status, wealth, and temperament of her employer.

Opposite, below: In Montana's sheep-grazing country, cooks were in great demand during shearing season.

to cut for winter hay and no wheat or corn with which to feed their families, many southwestern South Dakota homesteaders were obliged to find work wherever they could. According to Paula M. Nelson, most of the men in southwestern South Dakota worked in the mines or hired out to prosperous farmers in less arid areas of the state, leaving their wives to manage things at home. In addition to keeping the farm or ranch going in the absence of their husbands, many of the women whose children were old enough to be left alone all day went into town to seek work as housekeepers, nannies, or cooks—taking up the same work that had supported nineteenth-century pioneer women in the mining towns of the Rockies and Sierras.

Women's Work—for Wages

By the middle of the nineteenth century the majority of women who were employed outside the home were hired as domestic servants. Though "women's work" performed for others received as little respect as women's work performed at home, women—especially divorced or widowed women with children—were glad enough to have any paying work at all. And, poor as the wages were, for many single women, domestic work was the only honorable way to survive on the frontier.

In 1890, Emily French and her daughter Ollie moved in with the Frick family of Elbert, Colorado, and performed whatever domestic labors they were asked to do to help the family settle into their new home—cleaning windows, putting up "little white curtains," making pies and "some buiscuits," sewing aprons and frocks, and cleaning and sweeping. In exchange for her labors, French was given room, board, and enough cash to pay most of her other expenses. The work she did was often humiliating, and French describes it in great detail—right down to taking out the "slops" in the chamberpots and cleaning up messy beds. Some households paid better than others, and one, in particular, paid so little and demanded so much that French complained mightily to her diary, noting, "she must be crazy to ask me to do such a wash for such a price" and finally concluded: "She is an Irish Catholic, need I try to please."

Historian Lawrence de Graaf has noted that between 1850 and 1920, the four leading occupations of black women in the West were servant, laundress, dressmaker, and midwife. Clara Brown, a freed slave from Kentucky, charged fifty cents a shirt for the wash she did in Colorado mining towns, then used the money she had earned to invest in land. Within a few years, she had accumulated ten thousand dollars, which she used to search for a daughter who had been sold away from her in youth and to help other ex-slaves find work and homes in Colorado.

The scarcity of women in mining towns in the West meant there was always work for those willing to cook, clean, and wash, and Jerusha Merrill, a Connecticut woman who emigrated to California in 1848 with her husband and three children, declared, "a mans washing is no small item in this place it being onely from five to eight dollars per doz just diped in to the water and rung out at that." Noting that "female labour is above evry thing else," she declared, "Never was there a better field for making money than now presents itself in this place."

Missionaries, as well as miners, hired women as domestics. Eulalia Perez spent fifteen years as the *llavera*, or keeper of the keys, for the San Gabriel Mission in Alto, California, where she "tended to the enormous laundry, the wine presses, and the crushing machines which rendered the oil from olives." She was also in charge of the mission's commissary, handling the distribution of "tanned hides, chamois, sheep skins, Moroccan leather, flax handkerchiefs, nails, thread, silk."

Inevitably, women began to realize that there were other ways of turning domestic work to profit. Libby Smith Collins, who lost her home and all her possessions in a fire in Helena, Montana, decided to hire out as cook in a mining camp, a job readily available since most of the men in the

The Secret Bakery

Annie Green, who had two small children to tend and could hardly have afforded to work outside her Greeley, Colorado, home, still found a way to turn her work to profit. However, she quickly discovered that her husband made a clear distinction between her slaving over a hot stove cooking bread and pies for the family and doing the same thing in order to sell her wares to strangers. Green began her baking business quite by accident when a man who had smelled her fresh-baked bread knocked at her door thinking he was at a bakery, then asked if she would consider selling him a loaf anyway. When she realized that she could draw all the customers she could handle by turning out "larger loaves than any other person engaged in the business in town," she began to take orders for her bread and pies.

All of this had begun during one of her husband's frequent and lengthy absences from home, and remembering how adamantly opposed he'd been to her plan to take in boarders, she decided to keep her bakery business a secret for as long as she could. On the weekend her husband was expected home, she told her customers that her children would deliver their orders and that they were not to return to her door until Monday. With the last loaf delivered and the children safely home by the time of their father's homecoming, Green congratulated herself for her cleverness—until her little son piped up, "No I isn't going to tell papa not at all," after which it was only a matter of moments until her secret was out.

Annie was unwilling to give up work that had proved to be so profitable. "You believe in 'Woman's Rights,'" she told her husband, adding, "I claim that it is my right and also my duty to aid you when I can, without interfering with my household affairs." When he reluctantly agreed with that reasoning, she enlarged her business, and, since she had to keep a fire going all day in order to bake and wood was a precious commodity not to be wasted, she further supplemented family income by heating her flatirons on the glowing stove and ironing shirts for hire while her bread baked in the oven.

camp were "either unmarried or had left their wives and families in the eastern States." For seventy-five dollars a month she cooked for a camp of eighteen men from May to December, at which point she returned to Helena and married the owner of a nearby mine.

Pioneer Proprietors

For many pioneer women—married and single—taking in boarders provided a means of earning income while also maintaining a home. Mary Ellen Pleasant, a black emigrant to California, opened a boarding house soon after her arrival in San Francisco. An excellent cook and a hard worker, she prospered during the city's early boom days, providing room and board to a number of clients who later rose to prominence in California's business and political circles.

Libby Smith Collins recalled that her mother took in boarders in Denver at a time when the family was living in a tent and "our only table as yet was a large stump and our cook stove the camp fire." Even under such circumstances, feeding miners was a profitable business, for "even though food may not be served upon Damask table linen nor cooked upon a nickel-plated range, still it is a necessity at all times and places, and we found plenty who were satisfied to put up with the accomodations offered and pay therefor at the rate of $16 per week for meals alone." Through her mother's efforts, enough funds were raised to hire workers to help haul the logs and build their first home in the West.

Other women took housing and feeding miners a step further. Belinda Mulrooney, a single woman who made her fortune in the Klondike, established the Fair View Hotel in Dawson, outfitting it to the hilt—including "cut-glass chandeliers and silverware, china and linen and brass bedsteads," all of which were hauled in at great cost by pack train. Realizing that her hotel would not house a fraction of the people who were pouring into the area in the late 1890s, she decided to do her part to help meet the urgent need for housing. "I wasn't thinking of the money I'd make,"

she later recalled. "We just had to shelter those people." Whether or not money was her first thought, Mulrooney was soon one of the richest women in the Klondike.

Other women proved equally adept at other kinds of real estate ventures. After her husband, Clark, had worked for nearly ten years to acquire homesteads for himself and their children out west, Augusta Shipman finally agreed to leave Vermont and join him in Montana Territory, where she quickly managed to "prove up" all their holdings, something Clark had been unable to do in all his years of trying. Then, seeing "nothing but land out [t]here" on the open plains, Gusta prodded Clark into buying up more and more of it until "some 7 thousand acres were obtained," all of which was eventually sold at a sizable profit when the Great Northern Railroad came through the Judith basin.

Selling goods, not land, sustained still other westering women. In the years prior to her marriage, Abigail Scott Duniway talked a Portland merchant into allowing her to take twelve hundred dollars worth of goods on credit in order to open a millinery and notions store in Albany, Oregon. In three weeks she'd paid for the goods and was ready to take three thou-

sand dollars more on credit. Belinda Mulrooney made a small fortune by packing silks, hot water bottles, cotton goods, and other semi-luxuries in short supply into the Klondike, where she sold her wares for six times what she paid for them.

Boomtown Opportunists

Though relatively few in number, there were female prospectors in the West, some of whom were quite successful in the field. Mrs. E. C. Atwood, who gained an edge over her competitors by studying geology and mineralogy, eventually became vice president and general manager of the Bonacord Gold Mining and Milling Company of Colorado, and Delia McCarthy became president and general manager of the Cooperative Mining and Milling Company of Cripple Creek. Both the Silver Mountain Mining Company and the Clear Creek Mining Company near Denver were run by women, and another Colorado woman owned seventeen mines. With so many examples of success around her, Atwood told an assembly of the International Mining Congress of 1900 that mining could "be made to pay by any energetic woman who will pursue it in an intelligent way."

Left: *After running a series of hotels, restaurants, and saloons in Denver, European immigrant Katrina Murat and her husband moved to Virginia City, Montana Territory, and established the Continental, an elegant restaurant featuring gourmet foods, imported wines, and homemade pies and ice cream.*

Below: *Marguerite Greenfield, a feisty spinster, opened her own ice business in Helena, Montana, in 1912. When told that the trade was too hard for a woman, Greenfield replied, "I ride, swim, and row and do all things that keep one outdoors, so zero weather and a snowstorm do not affect me at all."*

Right: *A native of Nottingham, Ellen E. "Captain" Jack emigrated from England to the United States as a young bride. Widowed at thirty-one, she moved from Brooklyn, New York, to Colorado in 1880 and soon thereafter began prospecting near Gunnison. By 1882 she had gained control of the Black Queen silver mine, which she sold for $25,000—and which was ultimately valued at $43,000,000. In 1900 she built a cabin on a remote summit where she staked yet another claim. A published writer of poetry and prose, she was still living in that cabin at the time of her death at age seventy-nine.*

Right: *Wives of miners in the Pikes Peak region sometimes earned extra cash by taking in laundry, selling baked goods, or running boarding-houses.*

While Atwood and her Colorado colleagues chose an intellectual approach to mining, other women relied on hunches and instincts in their search for precious metals. Nellie Cashman, like many a male prospector, spent years following the strikes hoping to stumble upon a good claim that would assure her fortune. She supported herself in each new location by feeding hungry miners and supplying them with clothes and groceries. She ran a successful short-order restaurant in Virginia City, Nevada, in the early 1870s, then established a thriving boardinghouse in the newly opened goldfields around Dease Lake in the Cassiar district of upper British Columbia two years later. In 1880 she moved to the silver boomtown of Tombstone, Arizona, where she turned a fine profit operating a hotel called the Russ House and selling shoes, boots, and groceries at her Nevada Cash Store—until news of a gold strike on the Baja California peninsula sent her off on a near-fatal trek in which she and the other miners ran out of water and nearly died of thirst.

Even that close call did not dampen her enthusiasm for prospecting, and in 1898 she left restaurant and store behind and set out for the Klondike, struggling over

The Work of Women's Hands

the treacherous Chilkoot Pass and camping out in the snow until the ice broke up and the Yukon River opened to traffic. No stranger to boomtown economics, she promptly opened yet another restaurant and store, even as she began acquiring prospecting claims—one of which brought her nearly $100,000.

While Nellie Cashman never married and carried out most of her enterprises entirely on her own, Kate Mason Carmack,

a Tagish Indian woman, prospected in the company of her husband, George, and her brother Skookum Jim Mason. All three have, at one time or another, been credited with the August 1896 strike at Bonanza Creek that set off the stampede to the Klondike. After two years of mining their rich claims, the Carmacks went to Seattle to celebrate their good luck and visit George's relatives and friends. Afraid of getting lost in the corridors of the unfamiliar hotel in which they were staying, Kate used her hatchet to blaze a trail on its door facings and banisters, then she and George climbed out onto the roof and caused a near riot by flinging coins to crowds in the streets below.

Mavericks One and All

Mary Fields, a former slave who was born in Tennessee but ended up in Montana, was as quick with her rifle and revolver as Kate Carmack was with her hatchet. Six feet tall and weighing two hundred pounds, Fields had the reputation of being able to whip any man her size—even long past her fiftieth birthday. In 1884, after years of knocking about in the West, "Black Mary," as she was called by her neighbors, moved to Cascade, Montana, where she was hired by

Left: Single by choice, Nellie Cashman followed the strikes, hoping to hit a good claim while supporting herself by feeding and lodging miners in a successful series of restaurants and boardinghouses. She did particularly well with a store and restaurant in the Klondike— where she also acquired a claim that brought in nearly $100,000.

Below: Lucille Mulhall, who could rope from four to eight horses with one throw of the lariat, once amazed President Theodore Roosevelt by roping a coyote.

Lucile Mulhall Roping Four 5th Annual Round Up (Pendleton) — Moorehouse

Sharpshooter with a Mission

Martha Maxwell, a nationally renowned sharpshooter, zoologist, and taxidermist, began her career by hunting game with her husband. Known as the "Colorado Huntress," she brought down her quarry with a single well-placed shot—first having observed with great care the habits of the animals she stalked so she could pose them realistically in the taxidermy studio she set up in her home.

In 1873, when the city of Boulder offered her a hall in which to house her specimens, she opened the Rocky Mountain Museum, which the local newspaper described as housing "every beast of the forest and plains, every bird of the air." Eventually she moved the museum to Denver, and in 1876 her taxidermy specimens became one of the most popular exhibits at the Centennial Exhibition at Philadelphia.

Criticized for shooting so many birds and animals, she once argued, "Which is more cruel? To kill to eat or kill to immortalize?"

Right: Though hardly standard working garb, a bullwhip, angora chaps, and fringed leather gloves—plus a pistol painted in by the photographer—gave this turn-of-the-century cowgirl a fashion edge.

St. Peter's Mission to haul freight and help out with heavy chores. Armed with rifle and revolver, with a fat cigar clamped in her jaw and a whiskey jug at her feet, she got her loads through in all kinds of weather, sometimes managing a double load all by herself by driving a team of eight horses and pulling two wagons in tandem. She fought off wolves and thieves alike, never once losing a load to beast or bandits.

Unfortunately, Mary Fields was as volatile as she was reliable, and after she responded to an insult by a hired hand at St. Peter's Mission with a demand for a showdown with guns, the Bishop of Helena relieved her of her duties there. Moving into Cascade, Fields opened a small restaurant—but soon went broke because she gave away meals to those who were hungry but penniless. Less generous in her next business venture, she is said to have flattened with a single blow a customer who failed to pay his laundry bill. In 1895, well into her sixties, she began driving the United States mail, and her tireless, punctual runs through floods, blizzards, and mud were legendary. She died in 1914, having proven that the work of a woman's hands could be exceedingly varied.

Hispanic women, as well as blacks and

The Work of Women's Hands

Left: *Though not considered quite as outlandish as their nineteenth-century cross-dressing predecessors, turn-of-the-century women who donned men's clothing—even for hiking, fishing, camping and other outdoor activities—were still viewed as eccentric by most of their peers.*

Anglos, were pushing gender boundaries as they sought to make a way for themselves in the West. In the 1890s, Doña Candelaria Mestas, a native of northern New Mexico, carried the mail by horseback from Arabales to Rosa, New Mexico. Another unconventional Hispanic, Doña Gertrudis Barcelo, gained double acclaim as one of the best monte dealers in Taos and Santa Fe and one of the most astute businesswomen—or men—in the area as well.

Necessity often drove women to go to great lengths in order to take up jobs that were officially open only to men. In 1857, sixteen-year-old Elsa Jane Forest Guerin, a widow whose husband had been killed by one of the members of his riverboat crew, left her two children in St. Louis with the Sisters of Charity, donned male attire, and set out in search of work—and of her husband's killer, who had been set free on a legal technicality. Working first as a "male" cabin attendant on a steamer that ran the St. Louis–New Orleans route, she changed into women's garb once a month in order to visit her children. Though early on she gave considerable thought to giving up her male attire and trying to find a job as a woman, she never did, for, as she would later confess:

I began to rather like the freedom of my new character. I could go where I chose, do many things which, while innocent in themselves, were debarred by propriety from association with the female sex. The change from the cumbersome, unhealthy attire of woman to the more convenient, healthful habiliments of man, was in itself almost sufficient to compensate for its unwomanly character.

Lured by glowing accounts of the riches to be found in the West, Guerin joined an 1855 expedition to California but soon decided her strength was "[not] sufficient for the business" of prospecting. Work in a saloon eventually led to partnership in that enterprise, and the profits earned there led her to enter the freighting business, where she eventually earned enough money to return to St. Louis in style—only to find that she was bored by the genteel life her hard-won earnings supported. Donning male attire once more, she worked as a trader for the American Fur Company before trying mining again at Pikes Peak. Quickly giving up on that venture, she opened the Mountain Boys

Below: Showing no fear of the insects with which she works, this beekeeper wears no protective netting or clothing as she changes out the trays in her hives. Keeping bees not only helped farmers ensure the pollination of their orchards and fields but also yielded honey that could be used in lieu of sugar as a sweetener or sold at market to bring in extra cash.

Saloon, where she acquired the nickname "Mountain Charley."

Ultimately Guerin blew her cover by firing point blank at her husband's killer—who had the misfortune of wandering into her territory while on a trip out to Colorado. The man survived to reveal her identity but absolved her of all blame for attempted murder in return for her promise to let him go his way in peace. Perhaps her old enemy did her a favor of sorts, for when the bartender in her Denver saloon learned that she was a woman, he promptly proposed and she promptly accepted, giving up her ruse but maintaining the clothes and privilege she'd acquired as Mountain Charley.

Christened Charlotte Pankhurst at her birth in New Hampshire in 1812, another cross dresser, Charley Parkhurst, escaped from an orphanage as a young girl. Protecting her identity by living in barns with the animals she tended during a series of menial jobs across New England, Charley continued her masquerade after joining the 1849 rush to California, where she became a stagecoach driver renowned for her daring in racing her teams down

steep mountain trails at breakneck pace. Though she gained her place in local history through her exploits as a male and though she succeeded in hiding her true identity until 1879 when her secret was uncovered by the undertaker who prepared her body for burial, Charlotte Pankhurst was ultimately honored as a woman. She was, after all, the first woman to vote in a presidential election, having duly cast her ballot in November of 1868 in the little town of Soquel, California, where nobody had ever thought to question Charley Parkhurst's right to register and vote.

At Home on the Range and in the Fields

Other women took up "men's work" without assuming male identities. Sadie Austin, who grew up roping cows on her father's Nebraska ranch, decided life in the saddle suited her better than life in the kitchen and continued her career into adulthood. Ann Bassett, who managed cattle operations in both Colorado and Arizona, "could fit right in the toughest cow camp…take her place in the saddle with the rest and live the life they lived, doing with equal

skill her share of the work on the range."

Farming, rather than ranching, was the chosen career of a number of California women. Kate Sessions, a widow from San Diego, earned an international reputation for her horticultural efforts, and Emily Robeson gained fame with her nationwide olive business. An 1894 article in the *New York World* cited three Californians—Theodosia Shepherd, Georgia McBride, and a Mrs. E. P. Buckingham—for their success in running large agricultural businesses. Harriet Strong of Whittier did well enough raising oranges, walnuts, and pampas grass to become the first woman on the Los Angeles Chamber of Commerce. Strong also patented a "method and means for impounding debris and storing water" and went on to develop an irrigation and water company in California's San Gabriel Valley, thereby helping many other women—as well as many men—who were growing fruits and vegetables in the semi-arid regions of the West.

Pioneer Women Center Stage

Sharp-shooting pioneer women enjoyed great fame as stars in various Wild West

shows. Phoebe Ann Moses, a native of Ohio, began her career at age eight when she rested a long rifle on a porch railing and shot a squirrel. By the age of fifteen, she was supplying game to a Cincinnati hotel, and when showman Frank Butler came through the area and issued his customary challenge to the locals, the hotel keeper put his money on Annie—and won. A year later, Ann became Mrs. Frank Butler *and* Annie Oakley, the stage name under which she rose to fame as a member of Buffalo Bill's Wild West Show.

Though she did not win all her challenge matches, she was consistently accurate—once shooting 943 out of 1,000 glass balls—and she remained "America's sweetheart" even after more accurate markswomen—

Above: *A 1909 publicity photo of Jane Bernoudi, who was billed as the first woman trick roper.*

Left: *Phoebe Ann Moses, better known as Annie Oakley, rose to fame as a member of Buffalo Bill's Wild West Show.*

Right: Gambling was an adventure for women as well as men, and a number of females became quite adept at the gaming tables of the West—though most wore the fancy dresses of dance hall women, rather than the male attire sported by the daring and dapper cardsharp in this 1865 photo. Showing two aces, she's no doubt got at least one more up her sleeve.

notably Lillian Smith, a fifteen-year-old Californian who broke 495 of 500 glass balls—appeared on the scene. Dubbed "Little Sure Shot" by her fellow performer, Sitting Bull, Annie Oakley was ultimately immortalized in the Broadway hit *Annie, Get Your Gun.*

A St. Louis native who learned to ride, rope, and shoot on her family's 80,000-acre ranch in Oklahoma Territory, fourteen-year-old Lucille Mulhall weighed only ninety pounds, yet could "break a bronco, lasso and brand a steer and shoot a coyote at 500 yards." She could also "play Chopin, quote Browning, construe Vergil, and make mayonnaise dressing," though a *New York World* reporter noted that she was "a little ashamed of these latter accomplishments, which are a concession to the civilized prejudices of her mother."

Beyond the Bounds of Propriety

A 1903 Wild West show described by a Maryville, Missouri, newspaper as "the poorest ever seen in our city" featured Calamity Jane, a native of that state whose real name was Martha Jane Canary. A self-styled outlaw and hell-raiser, Canary was generally more infamous than famous—as were the other members of the short-lived Cole Younger and Frank James Wild West Show of 1903.

A woman who did all she could to sully her reputation in real life, Calamity Jane

laid claim to even more unladylike exploits in the memoir she hoped would assure her place in history. About all we know for sure about this undeniably colorful character is that she often drank to excess, did all she could to affront ladies in high society, and earned her living, in part, through prostitution. During the Black Hills gold rush of the 1870s, she worked a brief stint as a bartender, a scandalous act that so outraged "the good virtuous women" of Deadwood, South Dakota that, by her own report, a group of the outraged matrons came after her with a horse whip, intent on cutting off her hair. Whether or not such tales were

Above: *Fording the Dyea River was only one of many obstacles faced by these actresses on their way to the Klondike.*

Below: *Self-styled outlaw Martha Jane Canary was better known as Calamity Jane.*

true, they contributed to Calamity Jane's reputation as a woman who crossed beyond the bounds of propriety.

Prostitution alone would have put Martha Jane Canary in that category, for although bawdy houses were a fixture of almost every frontier town in the early days of the West, "soiled doves" were held in low regard by most proper women in western society. Not a few young women ended up in the "oldest profession" by default, starting out as domestic servants and ending up in a brothel after being ill-used by their employers. Others, notably Denver's Mattie Silks, seemed bound for the red-light district from the start, though Silks was always careful to point out that she began at the top—as a madam.

While madams like Mattie Silks prospered, their "boarders"—the census taker's standard designation for women of the night—often made just enough to sustain themselves, since they not only had to pay rent for their use of the premises but were also required to split each night's take with the madam. And, in a market where youth and beauty were ongoing requisites for monetary success, those less than lovely or past their prime could find themselves reduced to working the "cribs," a row of shanties with none of the comforts of even the lowest brothel and not the slightest pretext about their *raison d'être*. Depression was common, and many prostitutes drank to excess or sought the forgetfulness offered by laudanum.

As historian Mary Murphy has noted, there was a definite social order for prostitutes, and that order was determined by where a woman lived and worked. At the top of the Butte, Montana, hierarchy were the women who worked in luxurious parlor houses that offered companionship, entertainment, and a semblance of romance along with the sexual favors that were their primary commodity. Next were those who worked in shabby brothels furnished with secondhand chairs and beds and decorated with brewery calendars. And lowest in the order—and greatest in number—were the women who plied their trade in the "cribs" that lined the streets and alleys of the red-light district and where, in the words of one customer, "the whole thing, from the time you got in the room until the time you came didn't take three minutes."

According to Paula Petrik's study of prostitutes in Helena, Montana, though roughly half of that city's fifty-three prostitutes were Chinese as of 1880, there were no Chinese madams and most of the working women lived with "loafers"—the census taker's designation for pimps. Not surprisingly, these women fared poorly and Petrik notes that "in the social structure of the sexual marketplace, Helena's Chinese prostitutes were at the bottom."

Inhuman Bondage

According to multicutural scholar Ronald Takaki, the U. S. census lists "prostitute" as the occupation of 61 percent of the 3,536 Chinese women living in California in 1870. Many of the women so listed had been sold into prostitution by their own relatives. Only six years of age when she was first brought to San Francisco, Lilac Chen was told by her father that they were going to visit her grandmother, but instead, Chen recalled, "that worthless father, my own father, imagine…sold me on the ferry boat. Locked me in the cabin while he was negotiating my sale."

Wong Ah So was nineteen when a man told her mother that though he was only a laundryman, he earned plenty of money in America. "He was very nice to me," Wong Ah So recalled, "and my mother liked him, so…[she] was glad to have me go with him as his wife." Grateful to be wed to a man willing to take her "to such a grand, free country, where everyone was rich and happy," she was stunned to learn two weeks after her arrival in San Francisco that she was not the man's wife but his slave and that she would be working as a prostitute.

Soon after she arrived in California, Xin Jin was presented with a contract stating that she was to "voluntarily work as a prostitute at Tan Fu's place for four and one-half years for an advance of 1,205 yuan (U. S. $524)" to pay for her food and passage to the United States. If she caught one of "the four loathsome diseases," she must ask to be sent back home within one hundred days, after which time "the procurer ha[d] no responsibility." If illness caused her to miss more than fifteen days of work, she must work one extra month, and if she became pregnant, she would be required to work an extra year. If she ran away, she would be required to work as long as necessary to pay for "whatever expense [was] incurred in finding and returning her to the brothel."

A few prostitutes worked in high-class brothels where, according to Lilac Chen, "every night, seven o'clock, all these girls were dressed in silk and satin, and sat in front of a big window and the men would look in and choose their girls who they'd want for the night." Most, however, worked in shabbier establishments or "cribs"— 4 x 6-foot street-level compartments whose doors had barred windows through which the women peered as they called to prospective customers, offering pleasure for twenty-five or fifty cents.

According to historian Lucie Cheng Hirata, the women in the cribs were fed rice and a stew made of "pork, eggs, liver, and kidneys"—rations that cost their owners around "8 dollars per month or 96 dollars per year per person." A woman working the cribs earned an average of 38 cents per customer and serviced seven or more customers a day, thereby bringing in "850 dollars per year," for a total of "3,404 dollars after four years of servitude"—quite a handsome profit, since such women could be purchased from importers for as little as $530.

Mattie Silks, Madam Extraordinnaire

Even at the tender age of nineteen, Mattie Silks knew opportunity when she saw it. Inspired by the sudden influx of soldiers being mustered out of the Union Army, this enterprising businesswoman opened her first establishment—a modest and orderly Springfield, Illinois, house in which the boys in blue were welcomed with open arms by Silks and a host of young lovelies.

As the soldiers left town and business declined, Silks shut down that house and moved on to Witchita, a railroad terminus that was the destination point of hundreds of drovers. After a celibate six weeks spent driving cattle from Texas, the cowboys were more than ready for an evening's entertainment at Mattie's new house. Eventually Silks ended up in Denver, where she established a house that employed twelve alluring "boarders" and served fine food and choice liquor.

Most of Mattie Silks's profits, which were considerable, went toward the upkeep of twenty-two thoroughbred racehorses—and of a fancy-man named Cort Thompson. Though she had long been tolerant of Thompson's tendency to wander, upon hearing that he'd succumbed to the wiles of a rival madam, Kate Fulton, Silks challenged Fulton to a duel, engaged Cort Thompson for her second, and proceeded to the Olympic Gardens, a site just beyond the city limits and therefore beyond the town's jurisdiction.

When the smoke cleared, neither of the women bore a scratch—but the object of their affections lay on the ground with a bullet in his neck. There's no record of whose shot had done the damage, but as soon as Thompson recovered, he and Mattie Silks were married, a move that did little to improve her standing in Denver society but settled once and for all the question of whom Cort Thompson loved best.

Though those at the bottom of the demi-monde earned barely enough to survive, those higher up in the order sometimes had wages that exceeded those of the laborers and miners they served. Petrik's study of the bank accounts of seven prostitutes operating in Helena in 1880 revealed monthly incomes of $179 to $337, for an average of $233, an impressive sum when compared to the $90 to $100 that stone masons, bricklayers, and carpenters were earning each month or the $125 earned by bank clerks. And since the highest-paid saleswomen working in Helena's mercantile sector received only $65 a month, a woman who sold her favors earned nearly three times as much as one who sold clothing or candies or books.

In fact, according to Petrik, some women could—and did—earn enough as prostitutes to enable them to leave town and reappear elsewhere as comfortably situated "widows" eligible for love and marriage. Though she never married, Josephine Airey Hensely, the acknowledged queen of the madams of Helena's Wood Street district,

The Work of Women's Hands

later moved into real estate and enjoyed a fair degree of success before losing most of her money and dying penniless—but with all her mortgages paid up. During her relatively brief reign over Wood Street, Hensely, better known as "Chicago Joe," influenced the tone and focus of the city's sexual marketplace, leaving her mark in that one arena surely as other working women in the city left theirs in other spheres.

Indeed, the work of women's hands—whether in the form of unpaid domestic labor done to sustain a household; the unaccustomed toil of plowing fields, building fences, or panning for gold; the wage work of shopkeeper or salesclerk; the cooking and housekeeping endeavors of a boarding house operator; or the nocturnal activities of an enterprising madame—had its impact on the American West as surely as did the various and sundry labors of the men whose exploits have long been a part of that region's history and lore.

So, too, did the work of the relatively few pioneer women who entered various professions; the thousands of women whose volunteer efforts helped fund and maintain the educational, religious, and social institutions of frontier communities; and the dedicated corps of social and political activists who gave their all to eradicating vice, eliminating racism, and enfranchising women.

Left: To the women who worked in the bawdy houses, all men were basically equal, since the crumpled bills of a cowboy were worth the same as the crisp new bills of a well-dressed gentleman.

Opposite, below: An 1880s Denver parlor house operated by Belle Birnard.

Center: Chicago Joe Hensley, the acknowledged queen of the madams of the Wood Street district of Helena, Montana.

Below: Women of all races and creeds offered love for money to the men of the frontier. This Native American prostitute gained fame as "Indian Mary."

Molders and Shapers

Pioneer Women as Community Builders

In the West, as in the East, men held the economic and political power and therefore exerted considerable influence over the structure and operation of both rural and urban frontier communities. So evident was that influence that Utah pioneer Emmeline B. Wells admitted to attendees of an 1897 national suffrage convention that "[women] could not have settled Utah without [the help of men]." After all, she went on to explain, "They built the bridges and killed the bears." But, she added, "I think women worked just as hard, in their way."

"In their way" pioneer women were the molders and shapers of western society, slowly but surely exerting their influence on the cities, towns, and communities in which they lived. "Their way" did not mean "one way," for the community builders of the West were as varied in their attitudes, backgrounds, training, and methodology as were those of the East. Most often written into local and county histories were the accomplishments of the relatively few women who entered the various professions and made rather obvious contributions to community life as teachers, doctors, lawyers, and journalists on the frontier. Less often noticed and appreciated were the contributions of thousands of women whom sociologist T. A. Larson once called a "great mass of patient, modest, obedient, hard-working housewives," women whose volunteer efforts helped fund and maintain the educational, religious, medical, and social institutions of the West. The efforts of those quiet, behind-the-scenes workers were ultimately aided and abetted by the work of an equally dedicated corps of social and political activists who gave their all to eliminating racism, eradicating vice, and enfranchising women.

A Phalanx of Professionals

According to Larson, an 1890 *Special Census Report on Occupations* noted that 14 percent of the female work force in the West were in professional service of some kind, compared to only 8 percent in the country as a whole. And though the West had only around 4 percent of the nation's females, it claimed 17 percent of the female actors, 15 percent each of the female literary writers and of the female scientists, 14 percent of the female lawyers, 11 percent of the female artists and teachers of art, 10 percent each of the female doctors and of the female journalists, 7 percent of the female musicians and teachers of music, and a little more than 5 percent of the female professors.

There has been much speculation as to the reasons behind this phenomenon. Some have asserted that the West was more egalitarian than the East. Others have theorized that patriarchal patterns were less firmly established in a region that was defining itself as it went along, leaving women freer to pursue unorthodox goals. Some feel that once women realized they could drive a wagon or plow a field, they became more open to entering professional fields previously open only to men. Others opine that the scarcity of professionals of either gender on the frontier made it impractical to turn away women who offered essential services to pioneer citizens. Still others argue that western women entered the professions in larger numbers because women in the West were not

Opposite: Working through women's clubs and informal groups such as this 1910 Bible study class in Waterloo, Iowa, women across the West joined forces to fight for the many and varied causes in which they believed. From protesting the open sewers of Denver to closing down the red-light district of Seattle; from founding libraries and schools across Kansas and Nebraska to raising funds for a new church in Santa Fe; from protesting broken treaties with Indians in the Dakotas to pushing for safer working conditions and higher wages for miners in Butte; from battling demon rum in Oregon to rallying for woman suffrage in Utah and Wyoming, women were, indeed, the molders and shapers of the communities in which they lived.

While historians and sociologists differ as to the reason for the phenomenon, virtually all agree that by 1890 a larger percentage of western women were involved in professional careers than were their eastern sisters and that these women made significant contributions to the communities they served.

Frontier Teachers

The most popular professional career for western women was teaching, and though by 1890 a number of women were teaching in colleges and universities in the West, most women teachers were employed in the public and private grade schools and high schools of the region. Initially, many of the earliest teachers in the West had been trained in the East by nineteenth-century educators like Catharine Beecher and Mary Lyon, both of whom encouraged graduates of their respective seminaries to seek employment on the western frontier. In 1847, Beecher helped form the National Popular Education Board, whose objective was to inspire the surplus of single eastern women already trained as teachers to go west, and between 1847 and 1858 the board send out nearly six hundred women, each of whom was committed to two years of

Above, below, and opposite: *These Iowa teachers and British Columbia Catholic sisters taught domestic arts and moral precepts as well as academic subjects.*

denied entrance to the region's colleges and universities. The University of Deseret in Salt Lake City (later the University of Utah) was co-educational from its opening day, as were all other territorial and state universities in the West except for the University of California, which opened as an all-male system but admitted women a year later, in 1870.

Mission Schools—
A Mixed Blessing for Indian Children

Among the teachers in the West were those sent forth by various Catholic orders. In 1884, Sister St. Angela Abair of Toledo, Ohio, and five other Ursuline nuns traveled to southeastern Montana Territory and established the St. Labre Mission to the Northern Cheyenne Indians. They began teaching in a schoolroom furnished with a large table around which the children sat for their lessons—and for the late breakfast and early supper the sisters prepared for them. Soon thereafter, the operation was expanded into a boarding school.

Dedicated to the education and salvation of the children they taught, the sisters who labored in these and other mission schools across the West gave their all to their work, rising before dawn to attend to prayers, laundry, and baking duties, then putting in a full day in the classroom. When children were ill, the sisters took turns nursing them through the night.

Most mission schools—and most government schools as well—insisted that their students speak only English. Those who deliberately or accidentally spoke in their own language were punished, often severely. Operating in an era when acculturation and amalgamation were the ideals of all who worked with Native Americans, the priests and sisters in mission schools, along with teachers in Protestant and government schools, saw the loss of native customs and language as an indication of the success of their mission as educators. And most would have echoed Sister St. Angela's assessment of the parents of their charges: "Poor things! They are only overgrown children. A little fear has to be mixed with much kindness to lead them to God."

Fear of punishment was very real to Indian students, and Helena Sekaquaptewa, a Hopi, recalled how a teacher once damaged her hearing with a blow to the ear. Zitkala-Sa, a Yankton Sioux who attended the Santee Indian School in Nebraska in the 1880s, recalled how a "poor frightened girl shrieked at the top of her voice" after a beating. In her autobiographical novel, *Lakota Woman*, Mary Crow Dog recalled her grandmother's account of being beaten with a buggy whip for trying to run away from a mission school. As late as the 1950s, the school Crow Dog herself attended routinely beat students for "not doing one's homework or for being late to school."

Conversion to Christianity was a major goal of mission schools, and while some students readily converted to the religion of their white teachers, others did not. "The different sects were always urging and bribing us with little presents to join their church," recalled Helena Sekaquaptewa, "[but] it didn't appeal to me." Failure to give at least lip service to the beliefs espoused by a mission school could carry a harsh penalty, however, and Mary Crow Dog recalled, "I learned quickly that I would be beaten if I failed in my devotions or, God Forbid, prayed the wrong way, especially prayed in Indian to Wakan Tanka, the Indian Creator."

Such obvious ethnocentric bias has made it difficult for historians of religion on the frontier to assess the contributions made by mission educators. While there can be little doubt that Sister St. Angela and the hundreds of others who served in Catholic and Protestant mission schools were sincere in their concern for the welfare of the Native Americans with whom they worked, there is also little doubt that much of what was done in the name of helping Indians must, with hindsight, be recognized for the great disservice it was.

Above: *In 1851 the Cherokee tribe founded the first institution west of the Mississippi for the education of women. Located at Park Hill in what was then Indian Territory, Cherokee Female Seminary set high standards, recruiting its first teachers from Mount Holyoke Female Seminary. Destroyed by fire in 1887, the school was then moved to Tahlequah, where the spacious new complex pictured here was erected. "Fem Sem," as it came to be known, continued to thrive until 1907, when the attainment of statehood led to Oklahoma's takeover of all tribal educational institutions.*

teaching, after which she was free to remain where she was or to return to her home in the East.

Following her completion of the board's six-week tuition-free training session, twenty-six-year-old Mary Almira Gray bade farewell to her family in Vermont and joined a small group of teachers assigned to Oregon Territory. Sailing the Atlantic to Panama, the group was transported across the isthmus by steamer and flatboat to Gorgona, where they traveled on muleback to Panama City, some twenty-seven miles distant. Boarding a steamer there, they made their way to San Francisco and thence to Portland, where they were greeted and taken to various homes to await transfer to their assigned posts. Mary Almira Gray was sent to a school in Tualatin, and soon after finishing her two-year commitment, she married a local farmer, Benjamin McLench. Like many westering teachers, Gray not only made a professional contribution to the community in which she served but also made a personal choice—marriage—that bound her to the West.

Mary Almira Gray was among a relatively small number of teachers sent as far west as Oregon or California by the National Board. Most of the board's recruits went no farther west than present-day Minnesota. Harriett Bishop, one of twenty-six New England women who enrolled in Catharine Beecher's first preparatory course for teachers at New York State Normal School at Albany, eventually went to St. Paul, Minnesota, partly in search of adventure and partly because there were more openings for teachers on the frontier. Arriving there in the summer of 1847, she began teaching in a "mud and walled hovel" that had been a blacksmith's shop. By 1850 she and a friend from Ohio had established the St. Paul Seminary and boarding school, an institution dedicated to preparing teachers for employment on the frontier.

Unfortunately, relatively few of the young frontierswomen who aspired to become teachers had the advantage of studying in such a seminary. Some even presided over their first classrooms by default. During the early 1860s, school sessions in Little Falls, Minnesota, became so sporadic that fourteen-year-old Luella Fergus began holding at-home lessons for her younger siblings and seven or eight other children. Though her sessions ended when a Miss Camp—"a mere girl…[of] twenty" came to town at the start of the next school session, that brief introduction to teaching fueled her desire for a classroom of her own. Some months earlier she had written her father, James, in Montana Territory, that "Teaching school is all the talk among young ladies if they can do sums to fractions they can teach a school."

Though James Fergus had no objection to Luella's taking the local teachers' examination and preparing for a career in the classroom, he warned that she was too young to board out and teach in a school away from home, yet she must not accept a teaching position in Little Falls because "The children…[there were] too well acquainted with her" and she would find discipline too difficult. Advising her to be patient, he promised he'd find her "a school to teach" when she came west. Soon after her arrival in Virginia City, Luella did quite well as a substitute teacher in Rev. Thomas Dimsdale's school, but she married one of her mother's boarders before she could apply for a school of her own.

Bess Corey, a homesteading teacher in Stanley County, South Dakota, worked hard to improve her land *and* to improve the minds of her students. Until winter set in, she was walking the two miles between home and school twice daily. "Reached school with about as much life to build the fire," she wrote on a day when she'd sloughed her way through knee-deep drifts. Soon thereafter she gave in to the advice of her neighbors and agreed to abandon her home until warmer weather, concluding, "I can't wade snow four feet deep four miles a day and sit in school with wet duds."

In general, Corey's neighbors were helpful and friendly. When her outhouse blew over, a neighbor set it upright again; when her stove smoked and drove her outdoors, neighbors took her in until the stove could be repaired; they invited her to spend the holidays with them. It was not always easy, however, to be the center of such attention in a frontier setting where everyone knew everyone else's business. When the many single men in the area began to show an interest in her, Corey was flattered by their attentions but annoyed by the gossip stirred up by high bidding on her box lunch at the annual community fund-raiser. And, despite the many box lunches the young men bid on over the course of her teaching career, Bess Corey remained for the rest of her days "Bachelor Bess."

Teachers out west were often surprised by the facilities in which they were expected to operate. Angie Mitchell spent the fall of 1889 teaching in a brush-arbor classroom out from Prescott, Arizona. She was in the middle of a lecture one morning when she felt something tugging at her floor-length skirt. She looked down "and there lying on my…skirt in a ray of sunlight was as hideous a reptile as I've ever seen. He was black and yellow and tawny and had a body like a monstrous lizard and a 'spiky' looking tail and a head like a snake and was over a foot long." She hastily gathered up her dress "and with a yell one could hear a mile jumped on the stool" where she had been sitting. Upon learning that the visitor was a Gila monster that was unlikely to bite unless cornered, she ceased to be afraid and even "stroke[d] his scaly back with a pencil." Soon the lizard was coming back each morning, and Mitchell noted, "I've taken to picking him gingerly by the tail and putting him back of my desk where he lies out at full length in the sun and sometimes snaps up an unwary fly and seems to enjoy himself greatly. I've ceased to fear him tho' it will be long before I shall consider him handsome."

Below: Brush-arbor classrooms such as this one in Live Oak County, Texas, allowed an influx of cooling breezes while providing shelter from the broiling sun. And, as Angie Mitchell discovered while teaching in a brush-arbor school near Prescott, Arizona, such classrooms also provided many an impromptu lesson in the observation and identification of wildlife, as various creatures crawled, flew, or hopped into the welcome spot of shade.

PIONEER WOMEN

Right: Well into the twentieth century, midwives like Sybil Harbor of Lakeview, Oregon, filled an important niche in the health care systems of frontier communities.

Frontier Physicians

With doctors in such short supply on the frontier, almost every woman needed a modicum of medical skills, and many became quite adept at nursing themselves and their families through various illnesses and accidents. When thirteen-year-old Luella Fergus stepped on the blade of an ax while wading across a slough, she "cut her foot badly," so that "the red blood spurted." Fortunately, her mother, Pamelia, "hapen to bee their," for, as she later wrote James, "If the girls had of been alone I think Luella might have bled to death." Explaining that she "corded [the girl's] leg and sewed it up," Pamelia reported that Luella had been able to walk by resting her knee in the seat of a chair and hopping around on her healthy foot. Remarkably, perhaps because the wound had bled so freely, infection did not set in, and Pamelia concluded her report of the accident with a remark that serves as a reminder of how remedies and treatments were handed down from generation to generation: "If ever any thing of the kind happens [again],…[our girls] will remember this."

The skills of laywomen notwithstanding, there was a real need for well-trained physicians on the frontier. Thus Oregon pioneer Bethenia Owens was hardly prepared for the storm of opposition she encountered

when she announced that she was leaving her millinery business behind her in order to enter medical school. Persevering in her goal, she enrolled in the Eclectic School of Medicine in Philadelphia, an institution actively recruiting female students. When the school's major emphasis turned out to be hydropathy, or the treatment of illness through water, Owens supplemented her studies with lectures at Philadelphia's Blockly Hospital. Upon her return to Oregon in 1874, she passed through her hometown of Roseburg on her way to Portland, where she hoped to set up practice.

News of *Dr.* Owens's return was soon out, and a group of Roseburg physicians invited her to attend an autopsy—fully expecting her to decline and thereby show her weakness. When she accepted their invitation and showed up at the shed in which the procedure was to be performed, she was accosted by several male professionals who questioned the propriety of allowing a female physician to view an autopsy performed upon a male corpse. Furious, she demanded, "What is the difference between the attendance of a woman at a male autopsy, and the attendance of a man at a female autopsy?" Though no one answered her question, a vote was quickly taken and she was allowed to remain in the shed—at which point one of the doctors handed her his instruments and invited her to "do the

Frontier Doctor

Susan La Flesche was the youngest child of Joseph La Flesche, an Omaha chief. Sent east to study at a Presbyterian girls' seminary in New Jersey, she continued her studies at Hampton Institute in Virginia. When she was offered tuition assistance by the Women's National Indian Association, she entered Woman's Medical College of Pennsylvania, completing the three-year course in two years and receiving her medical degree in 1889 at age twenty-four, having graduated at the head of a class of thirty-six.

Following a year's internship at Woman's Hospital in Philadelphia, she returned to northeastern Nebraska to serve as physician at the government school for Omaha children. Soon thereafter she served for four years as physician for her entire tribe, an exhausting assignment that sent her traveling throughout the reservation on horseback. After her marriage in 1894 to trader Henry Picotte, she served both whites and Indians in the town of Bancroft, Nebraska.

work." Pulling aside the blanket, she made the initial incision, a scandalous act in the eyes of Roseburg's citizens—and one that effectively ended any hopes she might have had of practicing in her hometown.

In Portland Dr. Owens's hydropathy practice was successful enough to bring her a comfortable living and to enable her to put her son through medical school. Soon thereafter, she herself returned to the classroom, this time seeking a full medical education at the University of Michigan. Postgraduate study and clinical work were followed by a tour of European medical facilities. Upon her return to Portland as a specialist in diseases of the eye and ear, the forty-one-year-old physician married a second time, becoming Dr. Bethenia Owens-Adair, but continued her career until the age of sixty-five.

While Oregon women had to fight for the right to become doctors, women in Utah were welcomed into all fields of medicine and dentristy in the years following Brigham Young's 1873 suggestion that women's classes in physiology and obstetrics be formed in Salt Lake City and that the bishops should "see that such women be supported." In 1882 the Women's Relief Society founded Deseret Hospital, and Dr. Ellen B. Ferguson was appointed as its director. The hospital provided training in nursing and obstetrics for other Mormon women for some decades thereafter. As historian Sandra Myres has noted, by 1893, Utah still had the highest percentage of female physicians, but other western states were not far behind. Kansas Medical School, University of Oregon, and University of Michigan boasted female enrollments of 31, 20, and 19 percent, respectively.

Frontier Lawyers

Though fairly successful in their quests for medical degrees, women in the West had more difficulty obtaining legal training, since statutory prohibitions based on Roman tradition and English common law prohibited women from being called to the bar. The first woman admitted to the bar in the United States was Arabelle Mansfield

of Iowa, a graduate of Iowa Wesleyan who began her study of law by "reading" in a law office in Mount Pleasant. In 1869 she passed the bar exams so convincingly that one of her examiners noted that her responses to the questions on the exam had given "the very best rebuke possible to the imputation that ladies cannot qualify for the practice of law." Despite her landmark accomplishment, Mansfield never practiced as an attorney, choosing instead to teach English and history at the university level.

When Clara Foltz sought to practice law in California, she found her path blocked by a state law restricting the legal profession to "any white male citizen" who could pass the bar and meet certain moral standards. When Foltz wrote an alternative bill—the Woman Lawyer's Bill—which deleted the words "white male" from the original statute, a storm of outrage ensued in which many opposing voices questioned whether a woman lawyer should have to hear or elicit "indelicate testimony in court." Contemptuous of all such arguments, Foltz later recalled that "Narrow-gauge statesmen grew as red as turkey gobblers mouthing their ignorance against the bill, and staid old grangers who had never seen the inside of a courthouse seemed to have been given the gift of tongues and they delivered themselves of maiden speeches pregnant with eloquent nonsense."

Left: A native of New Hampshire and a magna cum laude graduate of Bates College in Maine, Ella Knowles moved to Helena in 1888 as a teacher but soon thereafter resumed reading law. Late in 1889, she became the first woman in Montana to take the bar exam—passing with one of the highest scores on record. In 1892 she became only the second woman in the country to seek the office of state attorney general. Running as the Populist Party's nominee, Knowles displayed such skill as a speaker that she was dubbed "the Portia of the People's Party." Though she lost to her Republican opponent, incumbent Henri J. Haskell, he soon appointed her his assistant attorney general, and before the end of his second term, the two were wed, giving reporters a perfect opportunity to remark once more upon the fact that politics does indeed make strange bedfellows.

Right: E. M. Clark
poses for what was
apparently a studio
self-portrait advertising
her Ruthven, Iowa,
business.

Below: An ingenious
self-portrait taken by
an unidentified photog-
rapher whose mirrored
image can be seen
above the cake at the
center of this festive
table.

Despite all opposition, the Woman Lawyer's Bill finally passed, and Clara Foltz became the first woman to be admitted to the California bar. She began practicing in San Jose in 1878, specializing in divorce and probate cases and accumulating a large clientele. A compassionate and understanding lawyer, she drew many clients who could not afford to pay for her services, and through her efforts, the state of California passed legislation saying that indigent clients were entitled to representation by a public defender, legislation that other states soon emulated.

Frontier Photographers and Journalists

In 1867 Mary Eckert, a widow, opened a studio in Helena, Montana Territory, billing herself as "M. A. Eckert, Artist," and cautioning the public that if a woman's picture "is not a lovely one, it will be owing entirely to the fact that, the original is not a beauty—and [is] not to be attributed to the camera, or the lack of skill in the artist." Despite her hard-line stance, Eckert outlasted many of her competitors, partly because she used her skills as a painter to enhance her photographs, offering "Pictures Colored, in Oil and Water Colors." Eulogized as "one [of] the finest operatives in the art," Eckert helped to doc-

ument the early years of statehood and left a valuable heritage in the form of photographs of many of the state's most prominent pioneers.

Montana's most famous female photographer of the pioneer era was Evelyn Jephson Cameron, an Englishwoman who first visited Montana in 1889 and moved to the state a year later. When her husband's financial situation tempted him to return to England, she persuaded him to stay and augmented their income by taking in boarders, raising vegetables, and selling postcards and albums of photographs she made using dry-plate negatives processed in her kitchen. Drawn by her naturalist husband's interest in birds and other wildlife, she took many memorable pictures of native fauna, as well as photographs that capture the beauty of the stark, magnificent landscape of eastern Montana and candid shots that depict men, women, and children in scenes of day-to-day ranch life.

While female photographers documented western life with their cameras, female journalists were both documenting

Mary Hallock Foote contributed illustrated articles on life in the West to magazines back east; Caroline Lockhart wrote a series of novels based on her interactions with the people of Cody, Wyoming; and Elizabeth Custer supplied eastern magazines with articles concerning her experiences as a military wife and recounted those experiences more fully in *Boots and Saddles, or Life in Dakota with General Custer*. Books written by Mary Austin Holley, Caroline Kirkland, Eliza Farnham, Laura Ingalls Wilder, and Bess Streeter Aldridge deal with life on the frontier, and many of the works of Helen Hunt Jackson, Mary Austin, and Willa Cather were based on their years in the West.

Left: *A California portraitist at work in Stockton.*

Below, top: *This threshing scene demonstrates the ability of British immigrant Lady Evelyn Cameron to capture everyday ranch life on film.*

Below, bottom: *A Mary Hallock Foote wood engraving,* Century *magazine.*

and influencing western life with their pens. Beginning in 1849, Amelia Bloomer established, edited, and published *The Lily*, an Iowa feminist journal whose editorials asserted the rights of women to enter any field they chose. In Utah, Louisa L. Greene founded the *Woman's Exponent*, a Mormon paper advocating the rights of women. Edited for nearly four decades by Greene's successor, Emmeline B. Wells, the paper served to keep its readers abreast of women's issues within the state and beyond. Oregon pioneer Abigail Scott Duniway ran the *New Northwest* from 1871 until 1886, and Caroline Churchill founded a Denver feminist paper, *The Colorado Antelope*, in 1879, changing its name to *Queen Bee* in 1882. Women journalists such as Leonel Ross O'Bryan—known to her readers as "Polly Pry"—achieved renown as reporters, columnists, editors, and feature writers for magazines, and in 1912 Charlotta Spears Bass of Los Angeles became editor of *The California Eagle*, the oldest black newspaper on the West Coast.

Right: *Guitarist Sadie Johnson-Ahrens, who rose to the rank of captain in the Salvation Army of Colorado Springs, was single and eighteen when she joined, serving alongside Ensign Rodgers, zitherist.*

Below: *Outside the Enright homestead near Glascow, Montana Territory, three members of the group described by sociologist T. A. Larson as a "great mass of patient, modest, obedient, hard-working housewives" engage in animated discourse on community affairs.*

An Army of Volunteers

The volunteer efforts of hundreds of pioneer women were the primary force behind the establishment, funding, and furnishing of the hospitals, schools, libraries, and churches in which frontier professionals practiced. In the words of one Colorado black woman, "women were the backbone of the church, the backbone of the family, they were the backbone of the social life, everything." So apparent was the impact of women as community builders in Virginia City, Nevada, that Louise Palmer, an early resident of that area, concluded, "The entire religious and social life of Nevada is conducted by ladies.

The lords of creation are mere money-making machines."

Similar patterns can be observed in the Hispanic culture, for, according to Fabiola Cabeza de Baca, the wives of *patrones*, the wealthy landowners, were, for generations, the primary community builders in the Southwest. "The *patron* ruled the rancho, but his wife looked after the spiritual and physical welfare of the *empleados* and their families," de Baca noted. "She held the purse strings, and thus…was able to help those who might seek her assistance."

While this fact might have been readily apparent to contemporaries on the scene, scholars have had difficulty verifying the work of women as community builders since no matter how many women worked toward the erection of a given building, generally only the men whose financial support would be crucial to its construction were pictured at groundbreaking and ribbon-cutting ceremonies and named in articles concerning the building.

There is at least one notable exception to this rule. Hallettsville, Texas, bears the name of the woman who opened that area's first store and was principal donor and sponsor for most of the community's enterprises. A forty-nine-year-old widow at the time she moved onto land her late husband had claimed on the Lavaca River, Margaret

Hallet offered her home as the site of district and county court sessions and as a resting place for circuit riders. She also donated the grounds for the Alma Male and Female Institute, a private school that was among the finest in the area.

A town was named in Hallet's honor, but she, like the men who've had buildings and towns named in their honor, made significant monetary contributions to the town and its institutions. What of the countless women who voluntarily contributed thousands of hours to fund-raising projects that helped build libraries, schools, and hospitals in Halletsville and all across the West? What has been done to immortalize Elizabeth Thorn Scott, the black woman who opened the first schools for her people in both Sacramento and Oakland?

And what tribute has been paid to the Native American women who constructed the lodges in which councils were held? Or to Anglo pioneers like May Wing, an unassuming woman who never bragged about her work or her civilizing mission but who, as she came to the end of her life, had a "few things [she was] kind of proud of," things she thought someone might, upon her death, "give…to the preacher and he could preach the story of my life"? That story would have included running the Victor [Montana] Museum, a task she began at age seventy and continued into her ninetieth year; helping to start the community's school lunch program; organizing a boys' chorus; and teaching in an ecumenical Sunday School she helped found. A short list, but one that should not be forgotten.

Neither should the accomplishments of various women's groups across the West. As historian Stephenie Ambrose Tubbs has noted, women on the Montana homestead frontier used their organizations a means of self-expression, and for many women of the era, self-expression meant community service. Founded in the late 1880s, the State Housekeepers Society of Bozeman, Montana, whose motto was "Our Kingdom Is Our Home," engaged in a wide variety of activities over the next century—from

A Founding Mother

In 1863, Sarah Burgert Yesler, whose husband was one of the founding fathers of Seattle, joined Asa Mercer, the first president of the territorial university, in planning and executing voyages organized to bring out from the East "a few hundred good women"—many of them Civil War widows—in hopes of improving the culture of the region and providing its many bachelors with prospective brides.

Having arrived in the Pacific Northwest at a time when Seattle was little more than a rude gouge in an otherwise unbroken expanse of trees, Yesler quickly began to make her presence felt. As her husband gained in financial and political stature, she gave her energies to the development of the settlement's cultural life, eventually making her mark as businesswoman, civic volunteer, and reformer.

She made frequent buying trips to San Francisco on behalf of her husband's store in Seattle, and became quite active in real estate. Yet her business dealings did not lessen her interest in civic affairs. She hosted the city's annual Fourth of July celebrations in Yesler Pavilion, which soon became the region's cultural center, a venue for Shakespearean drama and minstrel shows alike. By 1868, she was one of twenty Seattle residents on the board of the Library Association, and the town's library was, for a while, housed in Yesler Hall, with Sarah herself serving as librarian. In the mid-1880s, she became a founding member of the Seattle Ladies Relief Society, an early benevolence group whose projects included the Seattle Children's Home—particularly satisfying for Sarah Yesler, whose children had both died in Ohio (without a glimpse of the city their parents were so influential in building).

Also an activist, Yesler became a founding member of Seattle's Female Suffrage Society. One of four Seattle delegates at the state convention in Olympia in November of 1871, she served as temporary president of that convention. Over the years she hosted visits by Susan B. Anthony, Elizabeth Cady Stanton, Abigail Scott Duniway, and other suffrage leaders, often at Yesler Pavilion.

Upon Sarah Yesler's death at the age of sixty-five in August 1887, the flags in Seattle's harbor were lowered to half mast out of respect for a woman whose "unwavering faith in the growth of the city" had inspired others to give their energies to its development.

Above: *Belle Case La Follette speaks out for woman suffrage at a 1912 rally in Fox River, Wisconsin.*

collecting and documenting the state's early history to spearheading projects to improve lighting on city streets and in parks. The women of the Helena Improvement Society were dedicated to keeping streets and sidewalks clean, tending trees and footpaths, and establishing a city park system.

Dedicated to "individual growth and the direction of effort into lines of useful study," literary clubs often founded small lending libraries whose books were donated by local citizens. In many cases, these small libraries eventually evolved into town or county libraries housed in buildings club women helped to finance and staff.

Historian Paula Nelson notes that the Deep Creek Ladies Aid of southeastern South Dakota organized in 1908 to raise funds for the construction of a Norwegian Lutheran church. After several years, they contributed nine hundred dollars toward the new structure, which was built by members of the congregation. The Ladies Aid also purchased pews, the pulpit, the altar ring, the baptismal font, plus glass, paint, and other maintenance items. They supported the parochial school teachers, paid for the books used in the school, and were the most faithful attendees at services. "Without the ladies aid," Nelson concluded, "there would have been no church."

With "Lifting as We Climb" as their motto, the four chapters of the Montana Federation of Colored Women's Clubs (MFCWC) were active in improving playgrounds and housing for black citizens, as well as in doing their share toward soothing racial tensions during troubled times. As Susan Armitage and Deborah Gallaci Wilbert have noted, "the

rich club life of black women—church groups; literary, art, and musical groups; self-improvement societies; auxiliaries; sororities; and reform associations—was especially evident in the larger cities [of the Northwest]," and the records of individual clubs contain numerous accounts of the contributions these groups made to the communities in which they lived.

Often club records are a researcher's only means of discovering those contributions. For example, Elizabeth Thorne invited the founders of the American Methodist Episcopalian (A.M.E.) Church of Seattle to hold that church's first service in her restaurant, and soon thereafter the Ladies Social Circle raised the money to purchase a site for a church. Yet the official accounts of the building project list only the trustees of the church—all men.

A Brigade of Activists

Though the West has historically been regarded as the most egalitarian region of an inherently egalitarian society, an analysis of the opportunities the frontier afforded minorities—and women—raises serious questions concerning that time-honored assumption. Indeed, according to historian Rosalinda Mendez Gonzalez, "The history of the West, as the history of the United States, is a history of exploitation of the labor, land, and resources of diverse groups of peoples: Indians, indentured servants, black slaves, farmers, the working class, immigrants, and, not least, the exploitation of women in the home." Fortunately, there were nineteenth-century western activists who addressed some of these injustices by campaigning for the elimination of racism, the eradication of vice, and the enfranchisement of women.

As important as these reformers were in the shaping of the American West, they were not always accorded a hearty welcome by those in favor of maintaining the status quo. While acknowledging that a woman was "queen in her own home," Rev. Thomas Dimsdale, an 1860s minister, teacher, and editor of Virginia City's *Montana Post*, adamantly opposed any move beyond those sacred boundaries, declaring, "We neither want her as a blacksmith, a ploughwoman, a soldier, a lawyer, a doctor, nor in any such professions or handicrafts." While always ready to defend and revere "sisters, mothers, nurses, friends, sweethearts, and wives," whom he viewed as "the humanizing and purifying element in humanity," Dimsdale was equally ready to condemn those women who dared overstep their bounds and once importuned, "From Blue Stockings, Bloomers, and strong-minded she-males generally, 'GOOD LORD, DELIVER US.'"

His views notwithstanding, over the next few decades an impressive number of "strong-minded she-males" led vigorous and largely successful western crusades on behalf of minority rights, temperance, and woman suffrage.

Human Rights

As historian Susan Lee Johnson has observed, the West has historically been a place of "stunning racial and ethnic diversity, a diversity structured by inequality and injustice." And, according to historian Patricia Limerick, that very diversity "put a strain on the simpler varieties of racism.... forc[ing] racists to think—an unaccustomed activity."

With racist thought came racist legislation. Though both California (1850) and Oregon (1857) entered the union as free states, Oregon's constitution excluded the immigration of free blacks. And when the Fifteenth Amendment was proposed, both Oregon and California argued against its ratification, fearing, in the words of one *Oregon Statesman* reporter, that giving the vote to blacks would mean "we cannot deny the same right to the Indian or the mongolian." Indeed, neither Oregon nor California ratified that amendment, and in October of 1870, six months after the amendment was ratified nationally, Oregon formally rejected the amendment, using Southern arguments concerning the sovereign rights of states. Not until 1959 did Oregon consent to *symbolic* ratification of the Fifteenth Amendment, and California passed a similar resolution in 1962.

Oregon, California, and Nevada all passed laws against interracial marriage, and several western states passed laws maintaining segregation within their borders. There were laws imposing inequitable taxes on minority workers and laws justifying the appropriation of Native American- and Hispanic-owned lands by white settlers. In pre–Civil War California, it was illegal for persons of color to testify against a white person, and an 1854 California Supreme Court ruling by Chief Justice J. Murray made it clear that the exclusions of "Indians" and "Negroes" and "mulattos" from testifying applied to Asians as well. In 1879, 150,000 people voted to end Chinese immigration, while only 900 voted in

Below: The first convention of the Montana Federation of Colored Women's Clubs met in Butte in 1921. Black women all across the West found collective strength through membership in church groups and women's clubs dedicated to the improvement of life for all citizens.

Above: In the West, as elsewhere, the move toward racial harmony was often led by children.

opposition to that legislation. And, as historian Megumi Dick Osumi has noted, the California Constitutional Convention of 1878 declared that "no native of China, no idiot, insane person, or person convicted of any infamous crime" would be allowed to vote in that state.

In this allegedly egalitarian society, only in the Southwest—and then only in the very earliest days of Anglo settlement when there was plenty of work and too few laborers—was there a climate of tolerance for different races and cultures. As soon as the labor balance shifted, hostility toward the "other" emerged, shattering whatever racial harmony had, at first, seemed possible. Even so, as historian Martha P. Cotera has observed, for one brief moment—at the time Los Angeles was founded in 1781— there was a society so racially mixed that two of the wives of the founding fathers of Los Angeles were Spanish, one was "mestiza" (Hispanic and Indian), two were black, eight were "mulatto" (white and black), and nine were Indian. Such racial and cultural harmony had never happened in this country before—and nearly two centuries would pass before it happened again.

Many courageous women of different races have devoted their energies to addressing the inequalities and injustices that have plagued the West during most of its subsequent history. Mary Ellen Pleasant, a California realtor known as "Mammy" Pleasant, fought for the 1863 legislation giving blacks the right to testify in court,

then shocked the city of San Francisco by filing suit against two streetcar companies for excluding black riders. Charlotte Pyles, a free black living in Keokuk, Iowa, joined family members in raising funds to buy relatives out of slavery. In the 1850s, Pyles went on a speaking tour of the East in order to raise funds to convert her home in Iowa into a station on the Underground Railroad.

Susette La Flesche Tibbles, daughter of an Omaha chief and sister to Dr. Susan La Flesche Picotte, pled the cause of Native Americans to audiences in the East and in England. Known as Inshta Theumba, or "Bright Eyes," to her people, La Flesche was an effective spokesperson for Indian rights and helped set the stage for the passage of the Dawes Severalty Act of 1887 by which individual Indians were granted citizenship and were given portions of reservation land. And Sarah Winnemucca, a member of the Paiute tribe of present-day Nevada, played a key role in movements to preserve the lands of her people.

The Chinese who settled in the West in the nineteenth century could have used an advocate like Sarah Winnemucca, for these Asian immigrants suffered discrimination from the moment they entered the region. Ironically, as Patricia Limerick has noted, those who opposed Chinese settlement in the West did so in the name of American principals. A Mrs. Ana Smith declared, "They call us a mob. It was a mob that fought the battle of Lexington and a mob that threw the tea overboard in Boston harbor, but they backed their principles... .I [want] to see every Chinaman—white or yellow—thrown out of this state."

By 1882, though Chinese men who were students and merchants were still being welcomed into the country, Chinese laborers were no longer eligible for immigration and those who had come into the country prior to the passage of the Exclusion Act of 1882 were actively discouraged from remaining by the passage of laws forbidding Chinese women to immigrate to the United States. As Betty Lee Sung has noted, such government regulations "jumbled up family relations and mixed up family names" for decades. And according to Megumi Dick Osumi, the unbalanced ratio between Chinese men and women, when combined with antimiscegenation laws, made the establishment of a Chinese family in America all but impossible.

Labor Activists and Organizations

Anglo prejudice toward Chinese immigrants stemmed, in part, from the belief that the influx of Chinese workers was responsible for the shortage of jobs for Anglos and for the low wages being paid to railroad and textile workers. Thus labor issues were often intertwined with human rights issues, and activists were sometimes obliged to deal with both topics at once.

Numerous labor disputes arose in many mining communities, especially in the years after union organizers began to encourage workers to demand safer working conditions, higher wages, and better hours. Striking workers needed the support of their families, and Elizabeth Jameson's study of Colorado mining towns led her to conclude that the wives of miners "received public [recognition] for their toughness during strikes, much as women workers have been valued during wartime." Women acted as an untouchable force, yelling at the militia, throwing stones at soldiers, handing out strike-relief food and clothing—"things for which men would have been jailed or shot."

In strong union towns like Anaconda, Montana, there was never any question as to where a worker's loyalties should lie. "You didn't work without a union," recalled Katie Dewing. "You had your smeltermen's union, you had your carpenters' union, and your pipefitters' union, you had your waitresses' union, and *nobody* but nobody dared do anything against the union because then you were labeled a scab for the rest of your life." And, according to Claire Vangelisti Del Guerra, most people "felt that being a union person was vital to providing the right kind of conditions for you to work and also the right opportunities for you to make enough money to support your family."

In the years following the Civil War, women in rural communities began to take part in farm protest movements, becoming active in such groups as the Grange, the Farmer's Alliance, and the Populist Party. Some even joined the Socialist Party and the Farm Union, despite the fact that participation in labor organizations had heretofore been considered "a man's job." During the late 1920s, Montanan Verna Carlson became active in the Farmers Union, serving as Union secretary for seven years. And Anna Dahl canvassed northeastern Montana for the Farmers Union, striving to increase membership in the belief that a stronger union would mean improved farming conditions and better prices for farm products.

Below: When Labor Day was declared a federal holiday in 1894, pride in the businesses they'd built or helped to build inspired the women of Oakland, Oregon, to craft creative placards, don appropriate costumes, and take up the tools of their various trades as they joined in the city's celebration of its workers.

Above and below:
Members of the Women's Christian Temperance Union were not always of one accord in their fight against demon rum. Pictured at a Helena meeting in 1900, the staid and stalwart leaders of the Montana chapter of the WCTU would not likely have countenanced the bold demonstration staged by a group of Iowa women who touted the evils of liquor by lifting their beer mugs high in a "drink-in" of sorts.

Opposite, below:
Asked to pose for a photo during her stay in Wichita jail, Carry Nation knelt before an open Bible, saying this was her "usual attitude."

Temperance and the WCTU

Though conservatives sometimes criticized women involved in labor disputes for having entered into issues that did not concern them, few could deny that women who fought for temperance were fighting to protect the homes whose operation had long been considered their primary concern. Strong drink could turn an otherwise adequate, even amiable, husband into a violent abuser who was no longer able or willing to provide for his family. And in a region where miners, soldiers, railroad workers, loggers, cowboys, and merchants alike gathered with great frequency in saloons and taverns, Demon Rum was an easily identifiable target for those who

believed that strong drink was the root of this country's social evils.

In 1855 Bostonian Sarah Pellet arrived in California, intent upon supporting herself through temperance lectures. Dressed in bloomers, she had no trouble attracting crowds, and she offered a unique approach to the temperance issue: If the miners would outlaw liquor, she pledged, she would return to New England and gather up thousands of young girls who'd be more than eager to become the wives of law-abiding, temperate California men. Popular as Pellet's lectures were, she was unable to convince her listeners to trade liquor for ladies, and she made no discernible progress toward altering the saloon scene in the towns where she spoke.

Twenty years later, with the founding of the National Woman's Christian Temperance Union (WCTU) in Ohio in 1874, the movement to outlaw liquor took on renewed vigor under the leadership of Frances Willard. Daughter of pioneers who had emigrated from Ohio to Wisconsin by covered wagon in 1846, Willard had but four years of formal education before she went on to become head of a female seminary and an English professor and dean of women at Northwestern University at Evanston, Illinois. In 1879 she accepted the presidency of the WCTU, a post she held until her death in 1899.

A feminist to the core, Willard tried for years to make suffrage and other women's issues a part of the overall mission of the WCTU, but she was opposed by conservative members who made their views clear at the union's first convention by proclaiming, "We do not propose to trail our skirts through the mire of politics." Remaining firm in her belief that "every question of practical philanthropy or reform has its temperance aspect," Willard continued to push for a change in attitude, and under her leadership the national convention of 1880 endorsed the ballot for woman "as a weapon for the protection of her home."

In 1883 Willard took her lectures to every state and territory in the West, calling for reforms far beyond temperance and influencing many of the women who attended those lectures to take a more active role in the social and political issues of the day. Though Frances Willard died twenty years before the Eighteenth Amendment made temperance the law of the land and twenty-one years before she would have been able to cast a vote in a national election, under her leadership the WCTU had empowered thousands of women—many of them western women—who continued to battle for the reforms she had spent a lifetime championing.

By the time the country finally ratified the amendment declaring prohibition the

Here Comes Carry!

Carry Nation, one of the most famous warriors in the fight for temperance, had ample reason to join the crusade against liquor, for her first husband had been an alcoholic. Soon after settling in Medicine Lodge, Kansas, in 1889, she was urging her second husband, a minister, to denounce liquor from the pulpit, and a decade later she took her battle into the streets, walking into one of the town's rowdiest clubs while singing a temperance song. Shoved out onto the curb, she caught the attention—and the sympathy—of local citizens, and within a year had managed to close down all the bars in Medicine Lodge.

Moving her campaign to other towns, she armed herself with bricks and stones, smashing bottles, mirrors, and glasses with great gusto. Two days after Christmas in 1900 she launched an attack on the barroom of Witchita's Hotel Carey, a luxurious establishment with a curving cherry-wood bar, a sweeping mirror, and an oil painting of a naked Cleopatra at her bath. Shouting "Glory to God! Peace on earth!" Nation strode into the bar, heaved stones at the painting and mirror, then attacked everything within reach of the iron rod she'd hidden in her long skirt. Hailed as hero by many, denounced as crazy by others, she continued her physical attacks on saloons and bars, ultimately taking up the hatchet, the weapon for which she is best known, in a raid on Topeka's Senate Bar, watering hole of the state's legislators.

Clad in long black dress and bonnet, hatchet raised high against her foes, Carry Nation became one of the most famous women in America. But when she began selling souvenir hatchets and appearing in vaudeville stunts, she lost the approval of many, including Frances Willard and the WCTU, which refused to endorse her actions.

Carry Nation finally hung up her hatchet in 1911 at age sixty-four—eight years too soon to see the passage of the Eighteenth Amendment—and was buried beneath a tombstone that reads, "She hath done what she could."

PIONEER WOMEN

Below: Although Colorado defeated woman suffrage in a referendum held in 1877, in 1893 it became the first state in the nation to grant woman suffrage by popular vote. Here a group of newly enfranchised Denver women gather at the polling place.

law of the land in 1919, women like Frances Willard—and the infamous Carry Nation—had been giving temperance lectures for over sixty years. Ironically, forces that had little to do with the evils of alcohol were ultimately responsible for tipping the balance in favor of prohibition, for, as sociologist Alan Grimes has observed, by the time the Eighteenth Amendment was passed, a vote for prohibition had come to be seen as a vote against the German-American brewers of Milwaukee and St. Louis and a vote in favor of the wartime conservation of sugar. War-related sentiments aside, the Eighteenth Amendment would not have come into being had the WCTU not kept the nation's attention on temperance.

Suffrage at Last

Many of the earliest leaders in the temperance movement were also involved in the equally long and complex fight for woman suffrage. According to sociologist Alan Grimes, from its formal beginnings in the East at the Women's Rights Convention at Seneca Falls in 1848, the push for suffrage was closely interwoven with antislavery and temperance crusades and with broader issues of women's rights in

society, issues that had to do with "civility and reason supplanting the transitional rule of force and brute strength in society," issues generally associated with women as a "civilizing" influence on an otherwise rough and uncouth world.

Appropriately, perhaps, by the end of the nineteenth century, after fifty years of campaigning, the only four states to adopt woman suffrage—Wyoming, Utah, Colorado, and Idaho—were all in the "rough and uncouth world" of the American West. By 1914, eleven of the last eighteen states to be admitted to the Union had adopted woman suffrage—Wyoming (1890), Colorado (1893), Utah (1896), Idaho (1896), Washington (1910), California (1911), Oregon (1912), Arizona (1912), Kansas (1912), Nevada (1914), and Montana (1914)—while not one of the first thirty states in the Union had managed to pass a suffrage amendment.

While it is tempting to attribute this phenomenon to the fact that once a woman had shown she could drive an ox team across the plains and take on other chores in the male sphere, then men could not fail to give her the vote, enfranchising a group that held a clear majority was hardly something male voters would have done had they not seen the enfranchisement of women as something that furthered other important goals. And, as historian Julie Roy Jeffrey has argued, the first two territories to grant suffrage to women—Wyoming in 1869 and Utah in 1870—did so "not because women thought to ask for it, but because it suited a minority of men to give it to them."

Though there is some evidence that Wyoming feminist Julia Bright and her friend, Esther Morris, influenced Bright's husband, William, to introduce that territory's suffrage bill in the legislature, sociologist Alan Grimes asserts that the primary prosuffrage force at work was the need to stabilize a transient population and make the territory a destination point, rather than a place to pass through on the way to someplace else. In 1869, Wyoming Territory had a total population of less than ten

thousand and a ratio of six adult males for every adult female. Since most of those women had come west with husbands who were homesteading or involved in other long-term business ventures, granting the vote to women effectively doubled the votes of married men who had come into the region to stay, while weakening the votes of the transient mining population, most of whom had little or no interest in the territory's future. And, prosuffrage territorial legislators argued, enfranchising women would be likely to attract desirable female settlers, since women would come to view a move to Wyoming as a move toward political and social equality.

Once the state had made suffrage a part of its territorial constitution, its citizens remained firm in their suffrage sentiments. Indeed, when Wyoming petitioned for statehood in 1890, prompting antisuffrage U.S. Congressmen speak out against their suffrage laws, the territorial legislature wired Washington: "We may stay out of the Union for 100 years, but we will come in with our women." Whether because of—or in spite of—that show of unity and strength, Wyoming won the right to become the first woman suffrage state.

In Utah the suffrage movement succeeded primarily because the Mormon Church had two pressing reasons for enfranchising women—neither of which had anything to do with whether or not women deserved the right to vote. First, the territory was being threatened with Congressional action against plural marriage, and granting the vote to women seemed an excellent way of showing that the practice of polygyny did not make women slaves to the men they had married.

Second, passing a suffrage amendment meant increasing the power of Mormon voters at a time when the coming of the railroad and the discovery of several rich mining lodes had brought about an influx of "gentile," or non-Mormon, voters whose presence jeopardized the legislative plurality held by the founders of the territory. Utah, unlike the other territories, had had, from the start, an even distribution of the

sexes, for the Mormons were a family-oriented religion, and most of the men who had made the trek to Zion had taken their wives—sometimes *several* wives—with them. And, since the gentile miners and speculators were mostly unmarried men or men who had left their wives back east, enfranchising women diluted the gentile vote, while, in the words of Angie F. Newman, an early opponent of the church, "Every Mormon citizen…had his civil power extended in correspondence with his numerous alliances." Though voting records of the years following the 1870 enfranchisement of the women of Utah Territory would tend to bear that statement out, female voting loyalties became a moot question after the 1887 *dis*enfranchisement of the territory's women under the Edmunds-Tucker Act by which Congress sought to break Mormon control of the region. Past differences of opinion aside, Mormons and non-Mormons alike endorsed suffrage during the 1894 constitutional convention, and in 1896 Utah was admitted to the Union as a suffrage state.

Above: *The Cheyenne women in this 1888 engraving from* Frank Leslie's Illustrated Newsletter *were already experienced voters, for Wyoming Territory had given its women the right to vote in 1869. In 1890, when it seemed the woman suffrage clause in the proposed state constitution would cause the territory to lose its bid for statehood, the legislature stood firm on the issue nevertheless.*

Municipal Housekeeping

In 1926, Seattle became the nation's first large municipality to elect a woman major. Though that city had had its share of strong-minded women, Bertha Knight Landes herself rose to her post only after years of tending to business in "the woman's sphere"—dutifully putting husband, children, and church foremost in her life.

Easing her way into the public arena by gradually adding volunteer work and involvement in various clubs and civic organizations to her busy schedule as wife and mother, Landes practiced parliamentary procedure and honed her managerial skills as president of the Seattle Federation of Women's Clubs. From that highly visible post, she pushed for women's involvement in civic reform, proclaiming that "municipal housekeeping" was a natural outgrowth of the activities most women had carried on within the home.

Running for mayor on the premise that the skills, perceptions, and knowledge gained during years of running a household could be of great benefit to her in running City Hall and on the promise that she would bring women's values into city government, she was swept into office by people who had seen for themselves the contributions that she and other capable, civic-minded women had made to their communities.

Right: By 1912, the year she became the first Oregon woman to cast her ballot, Abigail Scott Duniway had already spent four decades campaigning for women's rights. As editor of the New Northwest *and as an officer in various women's clubs, she championed the cause of suffrage throughout the region. She managed Susan B. Anthony's 1871 tour of the Northwest and in 1884 was elected vice-president of the National Woman Suffrage Association.*

Other western states had equally complicated suffrage histories, but in every western—and eastern—state and territory the question of who stood to gain power and who stood to lose it held far more influence than the question of whether or not women were qualified to vote. Many strong and able suffrage leaders in the West—Margaret Campbell, Emma Smith Devoe, Luna Kellie, May Arkwright Hutton, and Abigail Scott Duniway—did their best to analyze all such questions as they threw their energies into the battle for the vote.

Politics—Not as Usual

Jeannette Pickering Rankin, an ardent feminist who had earlier gained the gratitude of thousands of Montana women during her long fight for suffrage in that state, had the support of many of her newly enfranchised sisters when, in the fall of 1916—four years prior to the passage of the Nineteenth Amendment—she became the first woman in the nation to win a seat in the U.S. House of Representatives. On her fourth day in Congress, Rankin, a staunch pacifist who always voted her convictions, joined fifty-six other legislators in opposing this nation's entry into World War I. After losing her bid to become the first woman to claim a seat in the U.S. Senate, she once more threw her energies into the suffrage crusade, traveling extensively on behalf of that cause until victory was gained on the national level in 1920. She also continued to work for world peace, serving as a member of the Women's International League for Peace and Freedom and as a Washington lobbyist for the National Council for the Prevention of War. In 1940 she ran again for the U.S. House of Representatives, and on December 8, 1941, became the only member of either the House or the Senate to vote against U.S. participation in World War II, a vote that, in effect, ended her political career.

What forces went into the development of a woman of such strong convictions? Might some of that courage and determination have come from growing up as the daughter of Olive Pickering Rankin, a New

Hampshire native who, in the summer of 1878, left family and friends behind and traveled west to accept a teaching position in Montana Territory? Might she have been influenced, as well, by western crusaders like Oregon's Abigail Scott Duniway? And, in turn, did Rankin's own success in politics inspire Bertha Landes to run for mayor of Seattle a decade later?

Clearly there were many influences at work in the lives of all these women. Suffice it to say that their own social and political "firsts" had been preceded by a number of other firsts, all of them serving as prerequisites for the political triumphs women like Rankin and Landes would eventually experience and all of them of interest in assessing the impact the West had upon women as well as the impact women had upon the West.

Though historians and sociologists are a long way from answering, in full, questions concerning whether or not moving west had a liberating effect on women, most are agreed that, at the very least, frontier living forced an end to the arbitrary divisions of labor that had limited their influence to the confines of the home. This is not to say that westering women who found themselves suddenly obliged to drive an unruly team of oxen across a sun-baked prairie or to plow new ground or herd cattle or do any of a thousand other chores that would, under other circumstances, have fallen to their husbands, fathers, and brothers considered such experiences particularly "liberating."

Yet even the most conservative westering women would likely have conceded that life in the West was considerably less confining—though sometimes less comfortable as well—than life in the East. Reluctant to move too fast into areas they were not yet sure they wished to occupy, the first generation of westering women were, according to historian Paula Petrik, considerably less likely to exercise their newly gained freedoms than were their daughters and granddaughters.

Those daughters and granddaughters—and even great-granddaughters—were the subjects of a 1943 Roper poll designed to

measure the attitudes and achievements of women of mid-twentieth-century America. As historian D'Ann Campbell's reexamination of that poll some three decades later revealed, "western women between the ages of twenty and thirty-five were better educated, evinced greater excitement and optimism about their futures, demonstrated a greater openness to change, and advocated equal moral standards for men and women more than their eastern, midwestern, and southern counterparts." Could this "western regional effect" have its roots in attitudinal changes that began when pioneers set aside old notions of the "proper place" for women in order to allow each sex to do all that was necessary in order to establish a home and earn a living on the frontier?

While the answers to such questions are clearly beyond the scope of this particular work, valuable clues to those answers lie within the words of frontier women who "lived the history [they] tell," women like Elinore Pruitt Stewart whose assessment of her experiences on the frontier serves as an inspiration to all women who have suddenly found themselves facing seemingly insurmountable obstacles: "I have tried every kind of work this ranch affords and I can do any of it."

Above: *In 1913, a year before woman suffrage came to Montana, aviator Katherine Stinson paid a visit to Big Sky country. As hundreds cheered from the midway below, her fragile biplane spun and sparkled in the bright blue sky above the state fair, a harbinger of all that was to come for women in the century ahead.*

BIBLIOGRAPHY

The stories told in *Pioneer Women* have been reconstructed from the letters, diaries, memoirs, oral histories, and other personal papers of the women themselves. In some cases, the authors have quoted directly from materials found in museums, libraries, archives, or collections held by families of pioneers. In many cases they are indebted to the work done by other scholars in the field who have published articles or books containing stories and quotations gleaned from their own years of research into the experiences of westering women.

To avoid burdening the reader with endnotes yet give due credit and references, the authors have cited sources by keying bibliographical entries to bracketed numbers in index entries for persons specifically named or quoted in the text. For example, to locate the source of a quotation by pioneer Angeline Mitchell Brown, look up Brown's name in the index, note the bracketed number in her entry [50], and match that number to the entry in the source list—in this case, entry 50, Moynihan, Armitage, and Dichamp's *So Much to Be Done*.

To find the source for information on a *topic*, rather than a person, note the name or names mentioned in the passage on that topic. For example, to find the sources for the discussion of the use of buffalo chips for campfire cooking that appears on pages 30–31 of the text, look up the index entries for the people specifically named in that discussion—in this case, Martha Gay Masterson and Stanley B. Kimball—then match the bracketed numbers in their index entries—in this case, [44] and [37]—with the numbered sources in the bibliography.

For sources whose index entry contains a bracketed seventy-nine—[79]—as a reference notation, refer to the photo credits.

The secondary sources that appear in the listing below are only a few of the many excellent articles and books being written by scholars in the field of western women's history. Though a comprehensive bibliography of such works has not yet been published, *The Women's West Teaching Guide* (item 28 below) compiled and edited by Melissa Hield and Martha Boethel and published by the Coalition for Western Women's History and the Sun Valley Center for the Arts and Humanities contains a fairly comprehensive list of sources, plus brief excerpts from many of the works cited. For ordering information, contact Susan Armitage, Women's Studies, Washington State University, Pullman, Washington 99164-4032.

1. Abair, Sister St. Angela Louise. Edited by Orlan J. Svingen. "A Mustard Seed in Montana: Recollections of the First Indian Mission in Montana," *Montana, the Magazine of Western History*, Spring 1984, pp. 16–31.

2. Anderson, Bertha Josephson. "Excerpted Material from the Handwritten Autobiograpny of Mrs. Peter Anderson, Sr., Sidney, Montana." Collection SC 360, Montana Historical Society, Helena, Montana.

3. Armitage, Susan. "Western Women: Beginning to Come into Focus," *Montana, the Magazine of Western History*, Summer 1982, pp. 2–9.

4. Armitage, Susan. "Western Women: A Centennial Quilt," in *Documents West*. An unpublished Washington State Centennial Project devised and edited by Stuart Grover (1989).

5. Armitage, Susan, Theresa Banfield, and Sara Jacobus. "Black Women and Their Communities in Colorado," *Frontiers*, Vol. II, No. 2, 1977, pp. 45–52.

6. Armitage, Susan, and Elizabeth Jameson, eds. *The Women's West*. Norman: University of Oklahoma Press, 1987.

7. Baxandall, Rosalyn, Linda Gordon, and Susan Reverby. *America's Working Women*. New York: Vintage/Random House, 1976.

8. Benson, Bjorn, Elizabeth Hampsten, and Kathryn Sweney, eds. *Day In, Day Out: Women's Lives in North Dakota*. Grand Forks: University of North Dakota, 1988.

9. Bishop, Joan. "Game of Freeze-Out: Marguerite Greenfield and Her Battle with the Great Northern Railway, 1920–1920," *Montana, the Magazine of Western History*, Summer 1985, pp. 14–27.

10. Blair, Karen J. *Women in Pacific Northwest History, An Anthology*. Seattle: 1988.

11. Brooks, Juanita. *Emma Lee*. Logan: Utah State University Press, 1984.

12. Campbell, D'Ann. "Was the West Different? Values and Attitudes of Young Women in 1943," *Pacific Historical Review*, August 1978, pp. 453–63.

13. Clappe, Louise A.K.S. (Dame Shirley). *The Shirley Letters*. Santa Barbara: Peregrine Smith, 1970.

14. Coleman, Michael C. "Motivations of Indian Children at Missionary and U.S. Government Schools, 1860–1918: A Study through Published Reminiscences," *Montana, the Magazine of Western History*, Winter 1990, pp. 30–45.

15. Cotera, Martha P. *Diosa y Hembra: The History and Heritage of Chicanas in the U.S.* Austin: Information Systems Development, May 1976.

16. Cowles, Florence Call. *Early Algona: The Story of Our Pioneers, 1854–1874*. Des Moines, Iowa: Register & Tribune, 1929.

17. Crow Dog, Mary. *Lakota Woman*. New York: Harper Perennial, 1990.

18. de Baca, Fabiola Cabeza. *We Fed Them Cactus*. Albuquerque: University of New Mexico Press, 1970.

19. Debo, Angie. *A History of the Indians of the United States*. Norman: University of Oklahoma Press, 1970.

20. de Graaf, Lawrence B. "Race, Sex, and Region: Black Women in the American West, 1850–1920," *Pacific Historical Review*, May 1980, pp. 285–313.

21. Dorset, Phyllis Flanders. *The New Eldorado: The Story of Colorado's Gold and Silver Rushes*. New York: Macmillan, 1970.

22. Faragher, John Mack. *Daniel Boone: The Life and Legend of An American Pioneer*. New York: Henry Holt, 1992.

23. French, Emily. *Emily: The Diary of a Hard-Worked Woman*. Edited by Janet Lecompte. Lincoln: University of Nebraska Press, 1987.

24. Furman, Necah Stewart. "Western Author Caroline Lockhart and Her Perspectives on Wyoming," *Montana, the Magazine of Western History*, Winter 1986, pp. 50–59.

25. Gray, Donna. *Four Women from Pray*. Readers Theatre (based on oral history interviews). Premiered March 15, 1989, Livingston, Montana.

26. Gray, Donna. *Nothing to Tell*. Unpublished oral history collection. Pray, Montana.

27. Grimes, Alan P. *The Puritan Ethic and Woman Suffrage*. New York: Oxford University Press, 1967.

28. Hield, Melissa, and Martha Boethel, eds. *The Women's West Teaching Guide: Women's Lives in the Nineteenth Century American West*. Sun Valley, Idaho: Coalition for Western Women's History and Sun Valley Center for the Arts and Humanities, 1985.

29. Hopkins, Sarah Winnemucca. *Life among the Paiutes: Their Wrongs and Claims*. Edited by Mrs. Horace Mann. Boston, 1883.

30. Horner, Patricia V. "Mary Richardson Walker: The Shattered Dreams of a Missionary Woman," *Montana, the Magazine of Western History*, Summer 1982, pp. 20–31.

31. James, Edward T., et al., eds. *Notable American Women: A Biographical Dictionary*. Vols. 1–3. Cambridge, Massachusetts:

Belknap Press of Harvard University Press, 1971, Vol. 1–3.

32. Jeffrey, Julie Roy. *Frontier Women: The Trans-Mississippi West, 1840–1880*. New York: Hill and Wang, 1979.

33. Jensen, Joan M. *With These Hands: Women Working on the Land*. Old Westbury, New York: The Feminist Press, 1981.

34. Johnson, Susan Lee. "'A memory sweet to soldiers': The Significance of Gender in the History of the 'American West,'" *Western Historical Quarterly*, November 1993, pp. 495–517.

35. Katz, W. L. *The Black West: A Documentary and Pictorial History*. New York: Doubleday, 1971.

36. Kaufman, Polly Welts. *Women Teachers on the Frontier*. New Haven, Connecticut: Yale University Press, 1984.

37. Kimball, Stanley B. *Historic Resource Study: Mormon Pioneer National Historic Trail*. National Park Service, U.S. Dept. of the Interior, May 1991.

38. Kittredge, William, and Steven M. Krauzer. "'Mr. Montana' Revised: Another Look at Granville Stuart," *Montana, the Magazine of Western History*, Autumn 1986, pp. 14–23.

39. Larson, T. A. "Women's Role in the American West," *Montana, the Magazine of Western History*, Summer 1974, pp. 2–11.

40. Lee, Rose. *The Chinese in the United States of America*. Hong Kong: Hong Kong Press, 1960.

41. Limerick, Patricia Nelson. *The Legacy of Conquest*. New York: W. W. Norton, 1987.

42. Luchetti, Cathy, with Carol Olwell. *Women of the West*. St. George, Utah: Antelope Island Press, 1982.

43. Malone, Ann Patton. "Women on the Texas Frontier: A Cross-Cultural Perspective," *Southwestern Studies*, Monograph Number 70, El Paso: Texas Western Press, 1983.

44. Masterson, Martha Gay. Edited by Lois. *One Woman's West: Recollections of the Oregon Trail and Settling the Northwest Country*. Eugene, Oregon: Spencer Butte Press, 1986.

45. Mayer, Melanie J. *Klondike Women: True Tales of the 1897–1898 Gold Rush*. Athens: Swallow Press/Ohio University Press, 1989.

46. Mercier, Laurie K. "'The Stack Dominated Our Lives': Metals Manufacturing in Four Montana Communities," *Montana, the Magazine of Western History*, Spring 1988, pp. 40–57.

47. Mercier, Laurie K. "Women's Economic Role in Montana Agriculture:'You Had to Make Every Minute Count,'" *Montana, the Magazine of Western History*, Autumn 1988, pp. 50–61.

48. Morrow, Delores J. "Female Photographers on the Frontier: Montana's Lady Photographic Artists, 1866–1900," *Montana, the Magazine of Western History*, Summer 1982, pp. 76–84.

49. Moynihan, Ruth B. *Rebel for Rights: The Life of Abigail Scott Duniway*. New Haven, Connecticut: Yale University Press, 1983.

50. Moynihan, Ruth, Susan Armitage, and Christiane Fischer Dichamp, eds. *So Much to Be Done*. Lincoln: University of Nebraska Press, 1990.

51. Mumford, Esther Hall. *Seattle's Black Victorians, 1852–1901*. Seattle, Washington: Ananse Press, 1980.

52. Myres, Sandra L. *Westering Women and the Frontier Experience, 1800–1915*. Albuquerque: University of New Mexico Press, 1982.

53. National Park Service. *The Overland Migrations: Settlers to Oregon, California, and Utah*. Handbook 105. Washington, D.C.: U.S. Department of the Interior, 1984.

54. Neithammer, Carolyn. *Daughters of the Earth: The Lives and Legends of American Indian Women*. New York: Macmillan, 1977.

55. Nelson, Paula M. *After the West Was Won: Homesteaders and Town-Builders in Western South Dakota, 1900–1917*. Iowa City: University of Iowa Press, 1986.

56. Oshanna, Maryann. "Native American Women in Westerns: Reality and Myth," *Frontiers*, Fall 1981.

57. Osumi, Megumi Dick. "Asians and California's Anti-Miscegenation Laws," in *Asian and Pacific American Experience: Women's Perspectives*. Edited by Tsuchida Nobuya. Minnesota: Asian Pacific American Learning Resource Center, University of Minnesota, 1982.

58. Peavy, Linda, and Sally Babcock, eds. *Canyon Cookery*, Bozeman, Montana: Bridger Canyon Women's Club, 1978.

59. Peavy, Linda, and Ursula Smith. *The Goldrush Widows of Little Falls*. St. Paul: Minnesota Historical Society Press, 1990.

60. Peavy, Linda, and Ursula Smith. *Women in Waiting in the Westward Movement: Life on the Home Frontier*. Norman: University of Oklahoma Press, 1994.

61. Petrik, Paula. *No Step Backward: Women and Family on the Rocky Mountain Mining Frontier, Helena, Montana, 1865–1900*. Helena: Montana Historical Society Press, 1987.

62. Reiter, Joan Swallow. *The Women*. (*The Old West* Series). Alexandria, Virginia: Time-Life Books, 1978.

63. Riley, Glenda. "American Daughters: Black Women in the West," *Montana, the Magazine of Western History*, Spring 1988, pp. 14–27.

64. Riley, Glenda. *Frontierswomen: The Iowa Experience*. Ames: The Iowa State University Press, 1982.

65. Roeder, Richard. "Crossing the Gender Line: Ella L. Knowles, Montana's First Woman Lawyer," *Montana, the Magazine of Western History*, Summer 1982, pp. 64–75.

66. Ross, Nancy Wilson. *Westward the Women*. San Francisco: North Point Press, 1985.

67. Russell, Don. *The Wild West or A History of the Wild West Shows. . .Before the Citizens of the Republic...Europe...the Globe...* Texas: Amon Carter Museum of Western Art, 1970.

68. Schlissel, Lillian. *Women's Diaries of the Westward Journey*. New York: Schocken Books, 1982.

69. Schlissel, Lillian, Byrd Gibbens, and Elizabeth Hampsten. *Far from Home: Families of the Westward Journey*. New York: Schocken Books, 1989.

70. Schrems, Suzanne H. "Teaching School on the Western Frontier: An Acceptable Occupation for Nineteenth Century Women," *Montana, the Magazine of Western History*, Summer 1987, pp. 54–63.

71. Sicherman, Barbara, and Carol Hurd Green, with Ilene Kantrov and Harriette Walker. *Notable American Women: The Modern Period*. Cambridge, Massachusets: Belknap Press of Harvard University Press, 1980.

72. Stewart, Elinore Pruitt. *Letters of a Woman Homesteader*. Boston: Houghton Mifflin Company, 1942.

73. Stratton, Joanna L. *Pioneer Women: Voices from the Kansas Frontier*. New York: Simon and Schuster, 1981.

74. Sung, Betty Lee. *Mountain of Gold: The Story of the Chinese in America*. New York, Macmillan, 1967.

75. Takaki, Ronald. *A Different Mirror: A History of Multicultural America*. Boston: Little, Brown, 1933.

76. Tubbs, Stephenie Ambrose. "Montana Women's Clubs at the Turn of the Century," *Montana, the Magazine of Western History*, Winter 1986, pp. 26–35.

77. Watson, Mildred. "Mary Wells (Granny) Yates." Manuscript in the archives of Gallatin County Pioneer Museum, Bozeman, Montana. Provided by Phyllis Smith, photo archivist, March 1995.

78. Wilson, Gilbert L. "Waheenee: An Indian Girl's Story," *North Dakota History*, Winter/Spring 1971.

79. See photo acknowledgements on last page of index for sources for the text for these captions.

INDEX

INDEX

ACKNOWLEDGEMENTS

The authors would like to thank the following individuals for their generous assistance and diverse expertise: Lawrence Christie, Ina Denton, Jan Dunbar, Donna Gray, Rivé Talbott Hoover, Kay Nordlund, Charlotte Orr, Kathie Otto, Phyllis Smith, Lydia Taylor, Lucille Thompson, and Dave Walter. Thanks are also extended to all the families who saved the letters, diaries, and journals of pioneer women and to all the archivists and librarians who have made those materials available to researchers and writers. Finally, the authors wish to thank Sara Hunt, whose vision began this project and whose patience, enthusiasm, and support contributed immeasurably to its successful completion.

The publisher would like to thank the following individuals for their advice, expertise, and assistance in the preparation of this book: LaVaughn Bresnahan, Rebecca Kohl, Shane Magalhães, Marty Miller, Ruth B. Moynihan, LaVera Rose, Kathey Swann, Michael Wurtz. Thanks also to the following individuals and institutions who supplied photographs for the following pages:
Archives Division—Texas State Library: 93; **Arizona Historical Society:** 74, 107 (top); **The Bettmann Archive:** 20, 21, 22, 23 (top), 31, 49 (top), 59 (bottom), 63 (top); Courtesy of **Lawrence Christie:** 76 (bottom); **Colorado Historical Society:** 105 (top), 136; **Denver Public Library, Western History Department:** 99 (bottom), 102 (top), 108 (both), 111 (top), 113, 114, 116 (both), 135 (top); **Douglas County Museum:** 133; Courtesy of the **Andrew Fergus family:** 7, 18 (bottom), 19 (bottom), 91 (both); Courtesy of **Rivé Hoover:** 44; **Idaho State Historical Society:** 6 (#60-139.13), 43 (#60-139.17), 48 (#60-72.43), 80 (top, #60-13926); **Lane County Historical Museum:** Page 9 (top), 72, 83 (top right), 84, 97; **Library of Congress, Prints and Photographs Division:** 1, 8, 9 (bottom), 11, 13 (both), 16, 18 (top), 19 (top), 23 (bottom), 24 (top), 32 (bottom), 33 (top), 50 (bottom), 52 (bottom), 63 (bottom), 65 (top), 71, 75 (top), 82, 111 (bottom), 113 (top), 130, 135 (bottom), 137,

138; **Local History Collection, Pikes Peak Library District:** 29, 60, 87 (top), 106 (both), 109, 110, 113 (bottom), 128 (top), back jacket; **Missouri Historical Society, St. Louis:** 36; **Montana Historical Society, Helena:** 4, 26 (top), 35, 46 (Haynes Foundation Collection), 53, 55, 58, 67, 68, 69, 73 (bottom left and right), 89, 101, 103 (bottom), 105 (bottom), 117 (top and center), 125, 127 (center), 128 (bottom), 131, 134 (top), 139; **Museum of New Mexico:** Page 96 (bottom), 27 (top, T. Harmon Pankhurst #8191), 30 (Keystone View Co. #91528), 64 (#108329), 96 (bottom #69106 Photo by Christian G. Kaadt); **National Archives:** 47; **National Archives of Canada:** 94, 121; **Nebraska State Historical Society:** 62, 132—**Solomon D. Butcher Collection:** 38 (top), 51 (top and bottom), 54, 76 (top), 78 (bottom), 80 (bottom), 86–87 (bottom), 132; **Nevada State Museum:** 66; **Oregon Historical Society:** 124 (#OrHi 23608); **Peter Palmquist Collection:** 10 (bottom), 62, 70, 73 (top), 78 (top), 81, 98 (bottom), 110, 112, 115, 117 (bottom), 126 (bottom), 127 (top); **Pueblo Library District:** 10 (top); **Sacramento Archives & Museum Collection Center, Eleanor McClatchy Collection:** 14 (top); **Sharlot Hall Museum Library/Archives, Prescott, Arizona:** 38 (bottom), 92, 96 (top), 99 (top); **South Dakota State Historical Society—State Archives:** 26 (bottom), 37, 45 (top), 49 (bottom), 50 (top), 59 (top left), 88, 95 (top), 103 (top), 120 (bottom); **Special Collections, Knight Library, University of Oregon:** 107 (bottom, Lee Moorhouse Collection, neg #M3780); **Special Collections Division, University of Washington Libraries:** 129; **State Historical Society of Iowa, Iowa City:** 77, 83 (bottom), 85, 95 (bottom), 98 (top), 100, 102 (bottom), 118, 120 (top), 126 (top), 134 (bottom); **State Historical Society of North Dakota:** 57; **State Historical Society of Wisconsin:** 79; **Western History Collections, University of Oklahoma:** 15, 52 (top), 104, 114, 122, 123; **Wyoming State Museum—Division of Cultural Resources:** 2–3, 40 (both), 56.